The
Emperor's Giraffe

The Emperor's Giraffe

AND OTHER STORIES OF CULTURES IN CONTACT

Samuel M. Wilson

Westview Press
A Member of the Perseus Books Group

Copyright © 1999 by Westview Press, A Member of the Perseus Books Group

Published in 1999 in the United States of America by Westview Press, 5500 Central Avenue, Boulder, Colorado 80301-2877, and in the United Kingdom by Westview Press, 12 Hid's Copse Road, Cumnor Hill, Oxford OX2 9JJ

Library of Congress Cataloging-in-Publication Data
Wilson, Samuel M.
  The emperor's giraffe and other stories of cultures in contact /
Samuel M. Wilson.
     p.   cm.
  Includes bibliographical references.
  ISBN 0-8133-3585-X
  1. Acculturation.   2. Culture diffusion.   I. Title.
GN366.W56   1999
303.48'2—dc21   98-55918
                                                                       CIP

Designed by Heather Hutchison

The paper used in this publication meets the requirements of the American National Standard for Permanence of Paper for Printed Library Materials Z39.48-1984.

10   9   8   7   6   5   4   3   2   1

For Cory, Nellie, and Marshall

Contents

Acknowledgments

Most of the essays in this volume first appeared in *Natural History* magazine, published by the American Museum of Natural History in New York. Some have been expanded from their earlier forms. They were published between 1990 and 1995 in a series titled "Worlds in Contact." The essays benefited from the excellent work done by the editors at the magazine, including Alan Ternes, editor in chief for most of the time these were written; Ellen Goldensohn; and Kay Zachariasen. I am especially happy to have space to offer sincere thanks to Senior Editor Vittorio Maestro, who edited all of the essays for *Natural History*. His thoroughness, patience, and commitment to making things as good as they can be are evident in this collection. I thank everyone at *Natural History* for their continued resolve to keep anthropology as an important part of the magazine.

Many of my colleagues in the Department of Anthropology at the University of Texas read versions of these essays. Emeritus professors Thomas N. Campbell and E. Mott Davis are both so widely read and interested in so many things that they were always excellent first readers. Ward Keeler went over nearly all of them in draft and gave them the kind of careful, detailed readings that, I know, is hard for professors to find the time to give. Polly Strong, Mel Tapper, James Brow, Tom Hester, Darrell Creel, Dorothy Lippert, Stephanie May, and others helped greatly on one or more of the essays. Chad Oliver died before most of these were written, but early on he told me that writing about anthropology for a general audience is more important than writing for other anthropologists. I value that advice.

A great many specialists in some of the specialized fields in which I have sometimes trespassed were very kind in providing information and advice. Without naming them all, I must acknowledge debts to Roger and Robert Abrahams, Vincent Hubbard, Tom McGovern, David and Joan Robinson, and Dan Rogers.

Cory Wolf edited and talked over all of these ideas and essays and made it all worth doing. I thank her most of all.

Samuel M. Wilson

Introduction

Twenty years ago, working at an archaeological site in the Midwest, I had the job of excavating a subterranean storage pit that had originally been dug and used more than 2,000 years ago. The pit was about two feet wide at the top, five feet deep, and four feet wide at the bottom. It had been dug by hand through the dark brown loam and down into a layer of soft tan clay. The only way to excavate it was to get down inside the pit as I dug and carefully remove its contents, bit by bit. It was a hot summer and the pit was airless. It took days of careful digging to figure out that the pit had been used for storage, then for garbage, and that layers of clay had been put down one upon the other to keep the rotting contents from smelling up the camp. Finally it was filled in completely. The top was eventually buried by the gradual accumulation of deposits; over the years the deposits at the site had built up to about two feet above the top of the pit. Inside the pit, near the end of this excavation, I began to clean the walls, right down to the yellow-tan clay. The brown organic contents of the pit flaked away from the soft clay revealing the finger marks of the person who had dug the pit a few hundred years BC. I put my right hand up to where the finger marks were and my fingers fit perfectly into the grooves. It is likely that only two people had ever been in the pit—the person who dug it and me. Across those millennia, I could feel a sense of kinship with a person with whom I shared at least the experience of a hot summer in the Midwest and a time in this hot pit (but probably much more).

In a way, the experience of excavating that storage pit was like trying to understand the reactions of people who were caught up in the

1

great period of culture contact that followed the arrival of Europeans and Africans in the Americas after 1492. Can we really experience the essential humanity of other people and the ways that they understood their times and their world across such a span of time and cultural difference? Some basic human bond of shared emotions and experiences is there, but at the same time cultural differences are real; we see the world differently, in ways that are determined by our culture. This makes the task of finding some of the human connections in the complex and chaotic history that has produced our world interesting and enjoyable, as well as important. One aim of this book is to search for these connections.

It is not difficult to argue that the world we live in is very different from the world of even a century ago. Obvious technological differences stand out, but there is also a major difference in the population of the world and its political organization. Far greater is the difference between our world and the world before 1492. The past five centuries can be seen as the time when people all over the world became much more aware of all of the others living in the world. In part, this was a consequence of the conquest of the Americas, but it also results from the global expansion of colonialism and changes in transportation and communication technologies.

The centuries since 1492 are marked by the processes of culture contact, perhaps more than at any other time in history. Groups who knew little or nothing of what went on beyond their islands or river basins were thrown, very often brutally, into a world of diverse cultures and agendas. These events resulted in a huge and rapid population loss in the Americas—and also the destruction of languages and cultural knowledge and experience. Other processes of culture contact took place over many generations, so gradually that individuals might not notice the kinds of cultural change that were slowly taking place. All cultures change constantly, reconstituting themselves in each generation. But in the contact period, cultural change has sometimes been violent, the result of forced assimilation or practices of exclusion.

The centuries since 1492 have also been a time of changing foundations for understanding the world and, generally, of increasing knowledge about the world. The Columbian voyages took place just at the time of the Renaissance in Europe—Michelangelo and Leonardo da Vinci were contemporaries of Columbus. Renaissance geographers like Prince Henry the Navigator of Portugal and the Italian Paolo dal Pozzo Toscanelli were interested in voyages like that of Columbus's small fleet. They were part of a process that has resulted, in the subsequent centuries, in the great dominance of scientific humanism as a paradigm for knowing what we know (or believe) about how the world and the cosmos work. Other aspects of Renaissance thought—the belief in the value and ultimate compatibility of different systems of thought and the innate dignity of humankind—do not at first sound like they had much to do with the period of colonialism and conquest that followed. They did play a key role in this period, however, which in the end was much more than a story of imperial conquest. The interactions in this continuing period of culture contact have changed all the participants—Europeans, Asians, Africans, and Americans.

In the essays in this collection, I try to focus on the way individuals understood their historical situation, but this is not easy in historical research. In archaeology, an experience such as the one I had in the storage pit is rare; it is unusual to see individuals so clearly. We deal, instead, with the homogenized artifacts made by many people and hope to get a kind of "average" view of what people were doing. We tend to look for longer-term trends—in population size, for instance—that take centuries to be clearly visible. This is the nature of archaeological data.

It is also somewhat difficult to see individuals in written history. Perhaps the most famous and notable people will be remembered for a few centuries, but most of us will not be. Eric Wolf wrote a very influential anthropological history titled *Europe and the People Without History* (1982). He sought to pull together the disjointed work of many academic disciplines in a new view of European history, one that avoided the problems of heroic "great man" genres of history. He noted, "Social historians and historical sociologists have shown that the common people were as much agents in the historical process as they were its victims and silent witnesses" (Wolf 1982:x). In many of the essays in this book, I have tried to follow Wolf's advice and look for the role played by people who generally do not figure prominently in traditional histories. The course of history is determined by choices and decisions people make, and not only those of the people whose names are recorded or remembered years later.

The idea that the course of history is determined by the decisions of individuals, famous or otherwise, runs counter to another prevalent view of history. This view is based on the assumption that the course of history is governed by powerful, unyielding forces much larger than individuals—the idea that at every moment outcomes are made inevitable by the onrushing succession of events. It is easy to feel this process in our world, faced as we are with frightening statistics about trends in population growth rates, the depletion of petroleum reserves, and global warming. Yet, as individuals we make our choices, informed by what information we have and in ways that make sense in terms of the cultural precepts we have learned since birth, and the result is . . . well, history.

Of course, the case might be made that the decisions made by some high-ranking people are more consequential than those made by anonymous persons in the crowd. This is often true, but as this collection of essays shows, it is frequently the other way around. Ordinary individuals find themselves, primarily due to chance, in situations of great moment. This element of chance, so prevalent in these essays, provides a second challenge to the view of history as a great juggernaut. It is rather unsettling to realize that the historical sequence of events could have been radically different at every stage.

In his book *Wonderful Life* (1989), Stephen Jay Gould asks readers to imagine the history of life on this planet as a tape that could be played back again and again to see if the course of biological evolution would always turn out the same each time. He argues persuasively that it would not; that at every turn, based on the paleontological record beginning shortly after the dramatic increase of species in the early Cambrian, chance played an enormous role in which taxa survived and which became extinct. Abrupt environmental changes, asteroid impacts, and other events brought about massive extinctions. One might counter that this result does make sense according to Darwinian principles of natural selection, making the case that the groups that became extinct were somehow inferior, but Gould argues that the pattern of extinction was random:

> Perhaps the grim reaper of anatomical designs is only Lady Luck in disguise. Or perhaps the actual reasons for survival do not support conventional ideas of cause as complexity, improvement, or anything moving at all humanward. . . . Groups may prevail or die for reasons that bear no relationship to the Darwinian basis of success in normal times. (p. 48)

Gould's argument is intended to apply to biological processes, but a comparable role of chance can be seen in human history. Play back the tape of the interactions between Europeans and indigenous people in the Americas and things might have gone differently at each point. Suppose, for example, that instead of the native peoples of the Americas being vulnerable to diseases from Europe, Asia, and Africa, things had been the other way around. If Old World populations had been decimated the way people in the Americas were, the world would be a very different place. As emerges from several of the essays in this book, the role of epidemic disease in changing the course of events in the colonial conquest of the Americas has been enormous, affecting native peoples, Europeans, Africans, and others. The point is not to explore large numbers of what-if scenarios or try to imagine all of the ways things might have gone differently; rather, it is important to see that chance events play an immense role in human affairs.

Especially in the first section of this book, which deals with the early European voyages to the Americas, it is easy to think of the "contact period" as something very remote, something that happened back in a period when history blurs into myth. The historical images of Columbus and Jacques Cartier and Sir Walter Raleigh are often placed in narrative settings that are in some ways very different from the history of Europe in the same period. Some historical figures have been made symbols for large parts of the population and responses to conquest (for example La Malinche in Mexico). Other people and events are bound up with religious faith, as in the case of Juan Diego and the Virgin of Guadeloupe. Other stories from this early period— Ponce de León and the fountain of youth, Coronado and the seven cities of gold, and even the Thanksgiving story of the Pilgrims—are more allegories than historical accounts. These are examples of a widespread belief in the Americas that the period of time encompassing most of the events of the early period of the European conquest is so historically remote as to be disconnected from the present.

Why do we put this distance between this contact period of history and ourselves? Perhaps it is simply that these events happened a long time ago and we are all a bit vague on the sequence of historical events. I think it is more likely that we distance ourselves because we know this history holds great sadness. Tragedies occurred that are almost unimaginable, together with crimes that are painful to contemplate and impossible to reverse. Yet in part at least, the world we live in is the product of these crimes and tragedies (as well as all of the positive things that happened). It is politically safer and emotionally less taxing, however, to blur history into myth and thereby confine it.

The problem with this strategy is that we are still in the contact period. If we see culture contact as the time in which different cultures interacted, exchanged, competed, and grew closer or farther apart—the time when they negotiated and engineered ways to live together—all of these things are still happening. The kinds of battles between nation-states, Creole landowners, and indigenous people that existed in the early sixteenth century are still being played out today. The conquest by force of indigenous people was going on less than a century ago in North America, and it is still happening in Amazonia. The political and social aftermath of the centuries of slavery is felt every day throughout the Americas. These wounds will take many generations to heal, and everything that happens after is premised on these events.

The intercultural processes that define the contact period also define the Americas. The societies of the Americas are typically far more heterogeneous than elsewhere in the world, and in fact this degree of cultural plurality was not common in history, even in large conquest empires such as the Roman, Aztec, and Ch'in (Qin). It is not possible to understand this diversity and the dynamics of these highly plural societies without understanding the long history of culture contact in the Americas, a history that began before the voyages of Columbus and continues to the present.

In the Americas, and particularly in the United States, there has been the belief that a fundamental process in culture contact is assimilation. Time and intercultural contact, in this view, work as a melting pot to erase cultural difference and absorb groups into a single, dominant culture. But there are a great many cases of cultural continuity spanning centuries that challenge this view. The Alabama-Coushatta people of east Texas, for example, came under serious threat from approaching Anglo settlers more than 200 years ago and survived by moving to Mexican territory. Their lands were incorporated into the Republic of Texas and then into the United States. Through much of this time they were under intense pressure to assimilate or leave—or die out. Today, as discussed in "A Texas Powwow," they are still doing well, living on the lands they have owned for generations. They have fought on the side of the United States in numerous wars and in most material respects are no different from their African-American, Anglo, and Latino neighbors in the Big Thicket of east Texas. But they are Alabama and Coushatta people. An essential part of their cultural identity remains unbroken through the years, even as most outward parts of their lives have changed. Trying to sort out exactly what that cultural continuity consists of is not easy, but ties of cultural identity have great strength and longevity. These people are one example of many that defy the melting pot idea of cultural change.

In the cultural complexity of our postcontact world, cultural identity itself is often very complex; for many people, checking a single box for "ethnicity" on a census form is impossible, as impossible as unraveling all of the complex lines of one's ancestry or sorting out all of the sometimes conflicting emotions of belonging. Many people, more in every generation, have ancestries tying them to multiple regions—Africa, Europe, Asia, and the Americas. How this is experienced can be seen in the chapter on Garcilaso de la Vega, who with an Inca mother and a Spanish father was one of the first generation of "mestizos" in the Americas. Twenty generations later, we are nearly all to some degree mestizos. As such, we are heirs to both aggressors and victims, with the additional complexity that brings. But in contrast to the melting pot view, recognizing this plurality of identity is not at all to say that we are without cultural identity.

Can we really understand one another across gulfs of cultural distance and long periods of time? Can we understand Garcilaso's reactions as the son of a Spanish nobleman standing in the ruins of his mother's Inca empire? Sometimes it is a daunting task to understand even part of what our friends are thinking and feeling, let alone strangers across space and time. I believe we can bridge these divides, and in this book I have tried to imagine things as they would have been for the people involved. Carrying on this search for common ground is another essential part of living in the contact period.

Works Cited

Gould, Stephen Jay
1989   *Wonderful Life: The Burgess Shale and the Nature of History.* New York: W. W. Norton.

Wolf, Eric R.
1982   *Europe and the People Without History.* Berkeley: University of California Press.

The
Columbus
Quartet

Even before the 500th anniversary of Columbus's landing in the Caribbean, most people were tired of hearing about him. If history were scripted for drama, Columbus would never have been cast in the lead. When historians wanted to make Columbus a hero (as they did in 1892, for instance), they had to gloss over a lot of historical facts and even make up whole plotlines to make him look good. The real Colombo or Colón (his surnames in his native Italian and adopted Spanish) was the sort of man who often cheated and bullied people. He tormented those from whom he wanted something and alienated nearly everyone else. As much as anyone in the early years of the conquest of the Americas—Native American or European—he was in over his head much of the time. In a sense, he was so fallible and human that it is perhaps fortunate he ended up where he did in history, if only because he is such a difficult person to romanticize.

The following four chapters dealing with the Columbian voyages and their aftermath have a lot to do with Columbus, but the focus also falls on some of the people around him. He found himself in competition with several Taíno rulers in the Greater Antilles, but for even longer periods he was allied with some of these men. As indigenous leaders suffering the first wave of European impact, they were dealing with awful predicaments, and they needed to figure out some way to read Columbus. It is hard to imagine that there was any real communication and cooperation across this huge historical, linguistic, and cultural divide, yet it was there. In looking at both sides of this exchange, however, it is tragic that so little of the Taíno's own views and ideas of the Europeans were preserved. One would like to know more of what they thought of Columbus.

Another group of people who figure in these chapters were Columbus's competitors and others involved in the endeavor to find a western, transatlantic route to the Far East. This was a big enterprise in the mid-fifteenth century, involving England, France, the Iberian kingdoms, and the large Italian city-states. To undertake a transatlantic venture a group had to gain the support of geographers, car-tographers, and other scholars for the project and then obtain government sponsorship, raise funds, and do all of the other logisti-cal things the voyage required. High-ranking people across Europe paid attention to these projects, as the correspondence in "Colum-bus's Competition" shows.

The times discussed in these opening chapters set the stage for many of the other chapters. The Columbian voyages and the events that followed did not seem like monumental events in Europe, at least not to the extent that we might think with hindsight. Euro-peans viewed the Atlantic venture as a part of an ongoing process of extending their sphere of trade and influence. They had long dealt with other people who were not like them in Africa, Asia, and the Is-lamic world, and they thought of the early encounters with the peo-ple of the Americas in the same way. These early interactions were to have great significance, however, and looking at Columbus and the people around him gives us a place to begin exploring the phenome-non of culture contact.

Columbus, My Enemy

In May 1497, the Taíno ruler Guarionex was enmeshed in a potentially disastrous political situation. Five years had passed since the strange and dangerous Spaniards first appeared on the northeast shore of Hispaniola. For five years Guarionex had attempted to mediate between the foreigners and his people and to maintain his power and prestige among the other Taíno caciques, or chiefs, who were sometimes his confederates, sometimes his competitors, in the complex political terrain of the Greater Antilles.

Two years earlier, Guarionex had witnessed the utter devastation the Spaniards could wreak in battle. Together with the other chiefs in La Vega Real—the largest, most fertile, and most densely populated valley on Hispaniola—he had set out to destroy the small force of Spaniards. Tens of thousands of Taíno, perhaps as many as one hundred thousand, had gathered from the largest chiefdoms on the island. They faced only about 200 Spaniards. But in battle the fury of the strangers had been awesome: Twenty men with armored clothing had ridden through his people on enormous animals, inflicting horrible wounds with their lances and swords. Men on foot used terrifying weapons that exploded fire. The Europeans' large dogs ran before them and with uncontrolled violence tore through the Taíno warriors. The Spaniards' goal seemed to be not merely to impress or subdue the Taíno or to embarrass the chiefs into joining them as subordinates but to kill as many people as possible. Even after the

13

battle they tortured to death some of the most respected chiefs in La Vega Real.

Soon afterward, however, the foreigners' ferocity strangely abated. They gave the remaining chiefs remarkable presents—glass beads, copper bells, brightly colored clothes. Faced with these powerful and unpredictable creatures, Guarionex had agreed that he and his people would be their subjects. From the Spaniards' signs and the few Taíno words they could speak, Guarionex understood that their leader, Columbus, demanded submission not to himself but to some even more powerful chief who lived on an island of which Guarionex had never heard.

Guarionex further agreed that his people would pay tribute in food, cotton, and gold. To placate the Spaniards, he offered to plant fields stretching for more than 100 miles, from the north coast of Hispaniola to the south. The Spaniards, however, appeared to want gold more than anything else: They demanded that every man of fourteen or more years give them one of their little copper bells full of gold every three months. Gold was relatively plentiful in surface deposits on Hispaniola, and although they valued it, the Taíno did not mine it extensively.

Still, the Spaniards required more than tribute. Because the Spanish ships came so infrequently and brought so little food, the colonists constantly roamed the countryside demanding the hospitality of the Taíno villages. Sometimes hundreds of Spaniards and the Indians that followed them would descend on a village for a few weeks. They called for food and seemed to eat much more than a Taíno would. And they did not eat just the food that was ready to be harvested; they also ate the manioc that normally would have stayed in the ground for another six months, and so after they left, famine followed.

By 1497, after two years of epidemics and famine following the arrival of the Spaniards, the other chiefs were pushing Guarionex to put up some resistance. Guarionex was a coward, they argued; groups of Spaniards who hated Columbus and his kin were living in Taíno villages and had promised to help the Taíno in battle if they would rise up again. The Spaniard Francisco de Roldán led a small army of dissatisfied Spaniards; he had told the chief Marque that he would help drive the Spaniards out of Concepción de la Vega, the fort that controlled the center of the island. Roldán promised that if the Taíno

Portrait of Christopher Columbus by Sebastiano del Piombo, "Christopher Columbus, 1519," The Metropolitan Museum of Art, gift of J. Pierpont Morgan, 1900.

won, the Spaniards would stop demanding tribute. His offer was attractive to many of the chiefs in La Vega Real. Most of them were subordinate to Guarionex in the Taíno hierarchy of social and political status, but their opinions were extremely important.

The Taíno world stretched more than 1,000 miles from east to west. Beginning more than 2,000 years before the arrival of the Spaniards, the ancestors of the Taíno had moved into the Caribbean archipelago from the northeast coast of mainland South America. They spoke a language (called Taíno) of the Arawakan family, one of the most widely dispersed languages in South America. By AD 700, after occupying the Lesser Antilles and Puerto Rico, they had pushed farther into the islands of the southern Bahamas and the western Greater Antilles—Hispaniola, Jamaica, and Cuba.

The ancestors of the Taíno were people of the tropical forest, who made their living by growing manioc and other root crops and by hunting, fishing, and collecting wild animals and plants. In the centuries of living in their new home, however, the Taíno way of life had become distinctively Caribbean. Ways of growing and collecting food had been adapted to island environments; social and political institutions had emerged that allowed a dense population to endure successfully in an island context. The sea served to unite, rather than separate, the Taíno. The elaborate oceangoing canoes of the chiefs could hold as many as 100 people, and voyages between islands were routine.

In addition to intermarriage between high-ranking lineages, the large chiefdoms of Hispaniola and the other Greater Antilles interacted with one another through a ball game. As in Mesoamerica and parts of South America, the Taíno played the game on large, flat courts lined with stones or earthen embankments. The game was played with a gum rubber ball, which could not be caught or struck by a player's hands or feet. For the Taíno, the game was much more than sport: It was a focus for religious festivals, feasting, trade, intermarriage, and the (relatively) peaceful resolution of conflicts.

Since the ancestors of the Taíno had moved onto the islands of the western Greater Antilles, the chiefdoms had been growing larger and more powerful. In 1492 Guarionex was one of the five most powerful chiefs on Hispaniola, ruling tens of thousands of people scattered over hundreds of square miles. All the villages of the central Vega Real—some seventy or more—were under his control through stratified tiers of less powerful chiefs. Most of his many wives had come from the highest-status families of these surrounding villages; his marriages helped forge the social and political bonds that held the chiefdom together. Some of his wives were from even farther away, from powerful lineages that ruled the other large chiefdoms of Hispaniola.

Among the Taíno, a chief's power was measured by his ability to convince others that his authority sprang from his birth into a maternal lineage of high status, his special relationship with supernatural spirits, and his political acumen. But his position was vulnerable; he could be deposed by his brothers or nephews or even by a member of another lineage. This Guarionex greatly feared. Despite misgivings that the rout of two years earlier would be repeated, he lent his support to the planned uprising.

Even as Guarionex was being pushed into battle by his confederates, Don Bartolomé Colón, Columbus's brother, learned of the impending uprising in La Vega Real. He had heard of Roldán's plan to join with the Taíno to take over the fort at Concepción de la Vega. If Roldán succeeded, the pro-Columbus faction would be cut in half—part would be in the coastal colony of Isabela and other forts in the north, part in newly founded Santo Domingo and other settlements in the south. Moving quickly with the 300 Spaniards he had with him, Bartolomé came into La Vega Real from the south. His men reinforced the fort, but they were still vastly outmatched by the surrounding Guarionex-Roldán alliance.

In many ways Bartolomé was the more capable of the Columbus brothers. He was described by Bartolomé de Las Casas, an important chronicler of the early contact period in the New World, as "a man who was prudent and very brave, more calculating and astute than he appeared, and without the simplicity of Christopher. He had a Latin bearing, and was expert in all of the things of men. . . . He was taller than average in body, had a commanding and honorable appearance, although not as much so as the Admiral."

As long as the Columbus family was the dominant Spanish faction of Hispaniola, Bartolomé was its de facto leader. He alienated members of rival factions to a lesser extent than his brother and interacted more effectively with the Taíno elite. In the two years since the first uprising in La Vega Real, he had learned to speak some Taíno and had developed relationships with many of the chiefs, in-

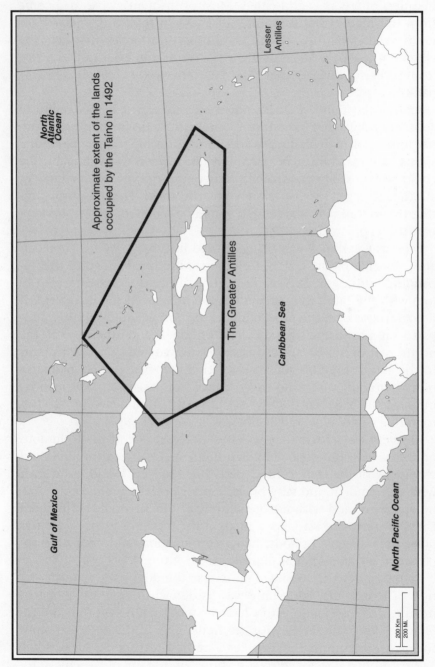

Map of the Caribbean, showing the extent of the lands occupied by the Taíno.

cluding Guarionex. He knew that the Indian leaders were becoming desperate.

As Bartolomé moved into La Vega Real, Guarionex and his confederates were assembling and preparing for battle. The allied chiefs were scattered in several villages within the central valley. The situation was different from two years earlier, when the Spaniards had so overawed the Taíno that no man could stand before them. Now the Taíno understood the power of the swords and horses, and the firearms had lost some of their terror. Moreover, they truly felt that they had no other hope but to defeat the Spaniards.

The force of fewer than 400 Spaniards at Concepción could not survive a determined attack by thousands of Taíno. The fort's small blockhouse could not even hold them all, let alone allow them to withstand a siege. In the morning, the Taíno would attack. Bartolomé realized that the situation was growing more dangerous by the hour. He had been drawn into fighting the Indians in the area where their strength was greatest, and if Roldán intervened, horses, armor, and firearms would offer little advantage.

In a breach of Taíno battle etiquette that was devastatingly effective for its novelty, Bartolomé staged a midnight raid on the surrounding villages. His plan was to capture many of the chiefs before they could attack in the morning. Small groups of horses rode into the villages and carried off fourteen chiefs before any defense could be organized. Bartolomé himself went into the large village of Guarionex and took the chief back to the fort. Las Casas wrote, "They killed many of the captured leaders, from those who appeared to have been the instigators, not with any other punishment (I have no doubt) except by burning them alive, for this is what was commonly done."

The raid threw the Taíno into chaos. Without their chiefs they were doubly lost. Their leaders not only directed warriors in battle but also mediated between the Taíno and supernatural spirit-helpers, who could bring them success. In the morning, according to Las Casas's account,

> Five thousand men arrived, all without weapons, wailing and very upset, crying bitter tears, begging that they be given their king Guarionex and their other leaders, fearing that the caciques would be killed or burned alive. Don Bartolomé, having compassion for them and seeing

*Engraving showing the battle between the Spaniards and the
Taíno in La Vega Real (from Antonio de Herrera,* Historia de
la Conquista de la Isla Española, *1762).*

their piety for their natural leaders, and knowing the innate goodness of
Guarionex, who was more inclined to put up with and suffer with tolerance the aggravations and injuries done by the Christians, rather than
think of or take vengeance, gave them their king and other leaders.

Compassion it may have been, but Bartolomé and his men were
still in the middle of thousands of desperate people, and Roldán was
still waiting in the wings. Bartolomé knew that without the political
organization the chiefs provided, the tribute system would quickly

collapse. Fate had cast Bartolomé and Guarionex as strange allies, each dependent on the other for his authority and survival.

This partnership, however, was fragile. Famine and disease were unabated in the villages, and among the Taíno the feeling of despair continued to grow. Guarionex was unable to protect his people from either the tribute demands of Columbus and the Crown or the unofficial demands for food and gold made by the anti-Columbus faction of Spaniards. Increasingly, Guarionex was viewed as a tool of the Columbus family, and his support from the other chiefs, from the pro-Roldán faction, and from his own people began to evaporate. He was able to maintain his position as a powerful chief for a little more than a year after the fourteen chiefs had been captured but then had to flee La Vega Real with his family.

Even then Guarionex could not find safety, because Bartolomé, fearing that Guarionex would return with an army, hunted him down in the mountains of northern Hispaniola, where he had sought refuge. Guarionex and his people had been hidden by Mayobanex, the most powerful chief in the northern mountains and perhaps a distant kinsman of Guarionex's. Bartolomé's capture of Guarionex brought about the destruction of this chiefdom as well, by the same strategy used elsewhere—capture the chiefs as hostages to ensure their peoples' tribute payments. Guarionex was held in chains at Concepción until 1502, when he was sent to Spain. His ship sank in a storm, and he died along with all the ship's crew.

The same forces that combined to bring Guarionex's rule to an end in La Vega Real were acting on all the other chiefdoms on Hispaniola and, ultimately, on others throughout the Greater Antilles. By 1500, most of the large political structures that existed on Hispaniola in 1492 had collapsed. For the Taíno, political disintegration and the decimation of the population occurred simultaneously.

The impact of the Europeans' arrival was felt differently on other islands of the Caribbean, just as it was in different parts of the New World. Ponce de León's conquest of Puerto Rico began in the early 1500s and quickly brought about the destruction of the Taíno way of life there. On Cuba the first Spanish attempt at colonization was less intense, in part because no gold was found and in part because the discovery and conquest of Mexico diverted the attention of Spanish fortune seekers. Indian populations there were not completely destroyed. In the eastern Caribbean, the Carib Indians were largely bypassed by early colonizers. Their descendants survive today as the Garifuna of Central America, although their preconquest island culture has been transformed greatly through five centuries of interaction with Africans and Europeans.

The indigenous societies of North, Central, and South America survived the arrival of Europeans with different degrees of success in what we have come to view as the remote contact period. Five hundred years, however, is a short fragment of human history. We are still negotiating the coexistence and synthesis of peoples with African, European, Asian, and Native American ancestries and heritages. Guarionex's struggle to retain his political status, to navigate the treacherous early years of the Spanish conquest, and ultimately to save his own life is just one story in this continuing process.

Works Cited and Suggestions for Further Reading

Dunn, Oliver, and James E. Kelly, Jr.
1988   *Diario of Christopher Columbus's First Voyage to America, 1492–93.* Norman: University of Oklahoma Press.

Las Casas, Bartolomé de
1951   *Historia de las Indias.* Mexico: Fondo de Cultural Económica.

Rouse, Irving
1992   *The Tainos.* New Haven: Yale University Press.

Wilford, John Noble.
1991   *The Mysterious History of Columbus: An Exploration of the Man, the Myth, the Legacy.* New York: Knopf.

Wilson, Samuel M.
1990   *Hispaniola: Caribbean Chiefdoms in the Age of Columbus.* Tuscaloosa: University of Alabama Press.

Wilson, Samuel M. (ed.)
1997   *The Indigenous People of the Caribbean.* Gainesville: University Press of Florida.

The Admiral and
the Chief

The news of the strange foreigners preceded them, but no one knew what to make of it. Were they gods, perhaps, or demons? Were they superhuman or only ordinary men of a type never before encountered? They had first appeared in the Bahamas in autumn and had gone from there to Cuba and then to the northwest tip of Hispaniola. As their two vessels gradually made their way eastward along the coast, they approached the region ruled by Guacanagarí, and the reports reaching this relatively minor cacique, or chief, of the Taíno Indians became more numerous. The foreigners' great boats seemed to be playing a strange game, going out to the little island of Tortuga and then coming back again. Even after they passed Tortuga, they continued to push far out to sea, and then come close to the land, as they progressed into the wind without anyone paddling.

Both Tortuga and the coast of Hispaniola were densely populated. Columbus, on this, his first voyage to the New World, described the lands he saw in his journal. His journal has been lost, but his experiences were retold in narrative form by the early chronicler Bartolomé de Las Casas:

> That big island [Hispaniola] appeared to be very high land not closed in by mountains, but level like handsome and extensive farmland, and all, or a large part of it, appeared to be cultivated, and the planted fields looked like wheat in the month of May in the farmlands of Cordova.

They saw many fires that night and, by day, much smoke like signals that seemed to be warnings of some people with whom they were at war.

The *Santa María,* Columbus's lumbering flagship, was a difficult vessel to sail into the northeasterly trade winds. She was not nearly so nimble as the *Niña,* the smaller caravel. (The expedition's third ship, the *Pinta,* had abandoned the others before they reached Hispaniola and had not been heard from for more than a month.) The winds were a tricky mix of the trades and on- and offshore breezes. Sometimes late at night the winds would die and the *Santa María* would drift on her own. The waters were unknown, and the dangers of hidden reefs and sandy shallows were always on the minds of the sailors. As winter pushed down from the north, it strengthened the wind patterns, and what are now known as the Christmas winds sometimes howled out of the east.

The slow progress of the strangers from west to east was gradually forcing Guacanagarí into action. How was he to deal with them? How could he avoid the problems they might bring, and how might they be used to his advantage? Whenever the ships anchored or even came near land, dozens of canoes would go to meet and trade with them. They would crowd together, canoe against canoe, until the Spanish ships looked like high points on small islands.

[Columbus] says he believes more than a thousand persons to have come to the ship at that hour, and all of them brought something of what they possessed; and before they reached a half crossbow shot from the ship, they rose to their feet in their canoes and took it in their hands what they brought, saying take it, take it. He believes also that more than five hundred came to the ship swimming because they had no canoes, and he was anchored nearly a league from land. . . . He ordered that something be given to every one, because, he says, it was all well spent; and, he says, may Our Lord in His mercy guide me so that I will find this gold, I mean the mine, since I have here so many who say they know it. These are his words.

The Taíno Indians of Hispaniola brought the foreigners food and water, parrots, weapons, cotton, ornaments, and gold. The Spanish sailors would trade what were, to them, less precious objects: old nails, bits of glass, coins of infinitesimal denominations, bits of brightly painted majolica pottery, small copper bells, and glass beads. The Spaniards' interest was clearly in gold; all their questions, as nearly as they could be understood by signs and a few words, concerned the source of the gold. Gold was also important for the Taíno. One of their words for gold had the same root as *cacique*, their word for ruler. In a strange parallel—one of many odd similarities between European and Caribbean cultures—gold, kings, and the sun were tied together in the same words and cultural categories.

For more than two months, Columbus had been searching for leads to the great cities of Cipangu (Japan) and the dominions of the Great Khan. He had abandoned his westward search along the north coast of Cuba because he and his crew felt the relentless trades forcing them farther and farther from Spain. In any case, contrary to the expectations Columbus had built from an ambitious reading of Marco Polo's travels, signs of what the Europeans considered to be civilized life seemed to be decreasing as they sailed westward. Everything pointed to the island of Hispaniola as the Taíno's cultural center and the source of their gold. And as the ships tacked eastward along the northern shore of Hispaniola, the evidence and stories of gold seemed to point to the interior of the island—to what the natives called the Cibao, a name close enough to Cipangu to warrant a closer look.

When the strangers came within the territory he controlled, Guacanagarí began to send envoys to invite them to his village. He sent the most precious and enticing gifts he had, including bits of gold and elaborately woven cotton belts. (These gifts, subsequently presented by the Spanish Crown to other European royalty, now lie scattered in European museums.) Ranking higher than other individuals whom Columbus had so far encountered, and perhaps standing on a point of protocol, Guacanagarí would not go to meet the ships but resolutely insisted that Columbus come to his village. Eventually, on December 23, Columbus and a large party of Spaniards did pay him a visit.

All of the Indians returned with the Christians to the village, which [Columbus] affirms to be the largest and best arranged with streets than any other of those passed through and found up to that time. . . . Finally the cacique came to them and the whole town, more than two thousand persons, gathered in the plaza, which was very well swept. This king was very courteous to the people from the ships, and each of the common people brought them something to eat and drink. Afterward the king gave to each one some of the pieces of cotton cloth that the women wear, and parrots for the Admiral, and certain pieces of gold. The common people also gave the sailors some of the same pieces of cloth, and other things from their houses, for small things that the Spaniards gave them, which, from the way they received them, seemed to be esteemed as sacred relics.

When Columbus and his people left the village, they gave the impression that they would soon move on. They pointed to the east, asking constantly about Cipangu or Cibao or the island's source of gold, and seemed convinced that it lay in that direction. They would move out of Guacanagarí's small domain and into the territory ruled by far more powerful caciques. The bizarre strangers, it appeared, would probably do him neither harm nor good. But Guacanagarí's fortunes, along with those of Columbus, took an unexpected turn.

It was Christmas Eve, a night on which, in spite of the date, the Christmas winds had died. Possibly a bit more wine than usual was opened, given the importance of the date to the Europeans. That and the long days of tacking into the wind and trading with the Indians may have made the pilot and those on watch somewhat less vigilant than usual. Columbus gave the helm to the ship's master, Juan de la Cosa, and went to his small cabin, about the only private spot on the *Santa María*. De la Cosa gave the tiller to a young boy and tried to catch a nap on a nearby coil of rope. The *Santa María* drifted ever so slowly on the current, with almost no wind. Columbus remarked that the sea was "as smooth as water in a bowl." The boy felt the rudder stiffen as the *Santa María* eased gently onto the sandbank. With an ebbing tide, her fate was already sealed.

A wooden craft the size of the *Santa María* can seem fairly light when afloat with a good wind, but on sand with the tide going out, it becomes impossibly heavy. Columbus ordered that the ship's boat be used to row the anchor some distance astern, so that they then could try to winch the ship free. Instead, the valiant sailors took off for the *Niña* with all the speed they could manage. Not permitted to board, they returned along with the *Niña*'s boat, but it was too late. In the middle of the night the *Santa María* creaked back and forth across the low swells; finally her timbers began to splinter as she broke up.

Diego de Arana of Cordova and Pero Gutierrez, two of the Crown's representatives among the crew, were sent to Guacanagarí's village.

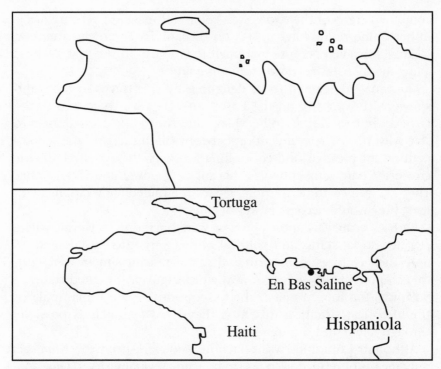

After Columbus's sketch map of northern Haiti, with a modern map of the region showing the location of En Bas Saline, a site thought to be that of Guacanagarí's village.

They were to enlist his help in salvaging the wreck and got a more positive response than they expected. Guacanagarí sent all the villagers and many large canoes to help ferry ashore the contents of the disintegrating *Santa María*. The crew were alarmed that all their goods, food, weapons, and wine might quickly and irretrievably disappear into the interior, but everything made it to land and to Guacanagarí's village "without a needle missing." Displaying sympathy in the Taíno's customary manner, Guacanagarí wept when he heard the news and "from time to time sent one of his relatives to the Admiral, weeping, to console him, saying that he should not be sorrowful or annoyed because he would give him all that he had."

The *Pinta* had abandoned the *Santa María* and the *Niña* before they reached Hispaniola and had not been heard from for more than a month. The *Niña*, despite a recaulking on Cuba, was still leaking. The combined crews of the two vessels could not make the return voyage in her. Some would have to stay on Hispaniola. Volunteers were not lacking, however, because many felt that a year on the island would allow them to stash away fortunes in gold.

Guacanagarí seemed to be delighted by this turn of events and showered hospitality on the Europeans. He gave them two of the large communal houses in his village and constantly pressed them to stay with him. The competition between Taíno caciques was a competition for prestige, and controlling access to these possibly divine creatures could only enhance Guacanagarí's power and social status. They all seemed to be warriors, possessing incredible weapons; with luck, they would become powerful allies.

Both Guacanagarí and Columbus were operating in worlds where elevated social status and political power were intensely desired. In both their cultures, high birth and personal achievement were critical components of success. And the birthright or inherited status of both was too low to match their aspirations. So both manipulated the historical situation in which they lived as much as possible, through talent and through luck.

Although Columbus was reluctant to debark from the *Niña,* his only means of returning to Spain, he made several visits to Guacanagarí's village. In the days they had together, despite a tremendous communication gap, the two developed a genuine rapport. Their futures were intermeshed now. Columbus's dream of reaping the benefits of a new trade route to the Orient depended on getting safely back to Spain with most of his crew and construing the wrecking of the *Santa María* as the successful establishment of a Spanish outpost in the Indies. (Calling his makeshift settlement La Navidad, Columbus had a small fort built from the timbers of the *Santa María*.) Guacanagarí's rising fortunes depended on a close and continuing relationship with Columbus. His small chiefdom could become centrally important in the Taíno world.

They needed each other so much that when Columbus returned a year later to find his small colony burned and all the Spaniards who stayed behind killed, he did not retaliate against Guacanagarí. The chief claimed that more powerful caciques than he had come to destroy La Navidad. But his account (which ultimately had several versions) was full of inconsistencies. The details of what really happened remain a mystery. Some of the Taíno had removed the Spanish presence by force. Perhaps the colonists' behavior proved intolerable; perhaps they introduced epidemics that the Taíno interpreted as punishment for upsetting the world order. Perhaps more powerful rulers wanted to return Guacanagarí to his subordinate status by doing away with the powerful strangers living with him.

In this first encounter between people from the New World and Old World, one of the most remarkable observations that can be made, with profound implications for the history of our species, is easy to miss. New World and Old World peoples had spent the previous ten to twenty millennia virtually isolated from one another. Since the ancestors of Native Americans crossed from northeast Asia some 12,000 years before, the two human groups followed their own paths and histories in near isolation. Yet in many ways the people of the Old World and the Americas were very similar. They lived in similar kin groups; they grew domesticated plants in the same ways; they both had domesticated animals; they lived in remarkably similar villages and cities; they had similar "governments" or political systems, similar hierarchies of social statuses; they both traded in markets; they had similar symbolic systems, writing systems, legal systems, myths, fears, hopes, and on and on. The words were different, but to a remarkable extent, the people of the Old World and the New World were speaking the same language.

The partnership between Columbus and Guacanagarí continued for several years after the destruction of La Navidad. At first, the chief and his people participated in the subjugation of the island, accompanying the Spaniards as interpreters and allies. But as Taíno society crumbled under the impact of Old World diseases and the demands of the Spaniards, and as Columbus was increasingly entangled in factional disputes among the conquerors, the alliance became obsolete.

Works Cited and Suggestions for Further Reading

Deagan, Kathleen (ed.)
1995   *Puerto Real: The Archaeology of a Sixteenth-Century Spanish Town in Hispaniola*. Gainesville: University Press of Florida.

Deagan, Kathleen A., and Bill Ballenberg
1987   1492 Searching for Columbus's Lost Colony. *National Geographic*, November 1987, v172, n5, p672–692.

Dunn, Oliver, and James E. Kelly, Jr. (eds. and trans.)
1988   *Diario of Christopher Columbus's First Voyage to America, 1492–93.*
         Norman: University of Oklahoma Press.

Las Casas, Bartolomé de
1951   *Historia de las Indias.* Mexico: Fondo de Cultural Económica.

Morison, Samuel Eliot
1991 [1942]   *Admiral of the Ocean Sea: A Life of Christopher Columbus.*
               Little, Brown (reprint edition).

Rouse, Irving
1992   *The Tainos.* New Haven: Yale University Press.

Wilson, Samuel M.
1990   *Hispaniola: Caribbean Chiefdoms in the Age of Columbus.* Tuscaloosa:
         University of Alabama Press.

Wilson, Samuel M. (ed.)
1997   *The Indigenous People of the Caribbean.* Gainesville: University Press
         of Florida.

Columbus's Competition

A few years ago I went on a modest quest in search of Paolo dal Pozzo Toscanelli, an archetypal Renaissance man and perhaps the foremost European geographer of the late fifteenth century. Toscanelli was convinced that by sailing west from the Atlantic coast of Europe, mariners could reach the rich trading centers of eastern Asia, and he encouraged Columbus and many other sailors to put the theory to the test. I wanted to see the astronomical device he designed for the vast dome of Florence's Cathedral of Santa Maria del Fiore to mark the summer solstice. Unfortunately, the bronze markers on the marble floor and windowsills upon which light and shadow fall were closed off by maintenance work, so to get a look at them I headed up the one-way staircase to the top of the dome. I thought that the markers would be visible from the balcony one had to follow around the inside of the dome.

Crawling up the cramped staircase and making my way through a stone tunnel out onto the balcony, I suddenly realized that I was at a dangerous height above the cathedral's marble floor. The balcony railing was only thigh-high (the great architect Filippo Brunelleschi's way of making the extraordinary dome appear even higher); things must have seemed safer to the children who were screaming and running around my knees. With my back against the wall, I made it around the balcony, crawled up the masonry caverns of the dome's ribs to the top, then back down to solid ground. (Toscanelli's markings were covered with tarps and I never did see them.)

Toscanelli lived at a critical time. Europe's population was growing rapidly, the feudal system of the Middle Ages was dying, and the Italian Renaissance was breaking new ground in artistic expression. A growing class of urban traders and artisans and a growing aristocracy demanded the silks, spices, and gems of the Orient. But the flow of goods along the land-based Silk Route had been stemmed by events in the Middle East: European relations with the Ottoman Turks had deteriorated, and the region was still feeling the effects of the expansion of the Mongol empire that had occurred in the preceding centuries. The most promising alternative to this overland route was by sea.

Among those with whom Toscanelli corresponded was Christopher Columbus, a merchant sailor from Genoa who had lived in Spain, Portugal, and elsewhere and who had been very active in Europe's expanding trade interests. Columbus had already been to Iceland and down the west coast of Africa. Now he was interested in finding a quicker route to Japan and China than the one the Portuguese had begun exploring around the southern tip of Africa. Believing, as did all educated Europeans, that the earth was spherical, in a letter Columbus recorded in his journal, Toscanelli encouraged Columbus's conviction that the fastest route from Europe to the Orient lay across the Atlantic:

> Paul, the Physician, to Cristobal Colombo, greeting. I perceive your magnificent and great desire to find a way to where the spices grow, and in reply to your letter I send you the copy of another letter which I wrote, some days ago, to a friend and favourite [Hernan Martinez] of the most serene King of Portugal before the wars of Castille, in reply to another which, by direction of his highness, he wrote to me on [the subject of sailing west from Portugal to reach the East Indies], and I send you another sea chart like the one I sent him, by which you will be satisfied respecting your enquiries.

Toscanelli's instructions were not confidential: He had been spreading this message for quite a while before his correspondence with Columbus. As early as 1474 he had exchanged letters with a Portuguese cleric attached to the Portuguese court and had recommended this western route over the proposed route around Africa, saying it was "a shorter way of going by sea to the lands of spices."

Columbus did not have any particular advantage over his competition. His ships were no better, and possibly worse. He based his understanding of the shape of the world on information that everyone

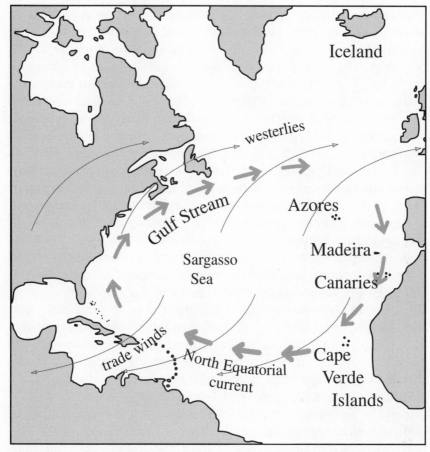

The Atlantic Ocean, showing the Atlantic islands and the major currents and winds affecting navigation.

else had access to. (Perhaps to his advantage, he interpreted this meager information incorrectly: He thought the world was much smaller than it was.) So why did Columbus reach the New World ahead of his competitors? In part because of a few shrewd decisions, and to a large extent because of luck. Perhaps his most critical, or luckiest, decision was to sail by way of the more southerly Canary Islands instead of the Azores.

In the mythical versions of Columbus's first voyage, the vast and sinister Atlantic Ocean was completely uncharted, and Europeans left sight of land at their peril. In fact, islands lying far out in the North

Atlantic were already known. Key to their discovery was the pattern of winds and currents off the African and European coasts. Ocean currents flow in a clockwise direction around the North Atlantic's perimeter: The Canaries current flows down the coast of Europe to the bulge of West Africa, the northern equatorial current crosses the Atlantic along the Tropic of Cancer, and the Gulf Stream races up the eastern seaboard of North America and then drifts across to Europe. Its waters help to keep the United Kingdom's climate relatively mild, even though all of the British islands lie farther to the north than any part of the continental United States. The winds push these currents along: The trade winds blow from east to west on the southern part of the circle and the westerlies bring the currents back to Europe.

Thus, sailing down the west coast of Africa was not difficult for fifteenth-century European navigators. The Canaries current and the trade winds were in their favor. On the return trip, however, they had to fight both winds and ocean currents. Portuguese mariners did two things to get around these obstacles. First, they built small, agile ships, called caravels, that could sail into the wind more easily and still take the Atlantic's pounding (Columbus's *Niña* and *Pinta* were examples). Second, they sailed west into the Atlantic, away from the coast-hugging Canaries current, before turning north. As a result, they found the Cape Verde Islands, the Madeiras, and the Azores.

From the late 1470s to the mid-1480s, Columbus himself lived on one of the Madeiras, more than 500 miles from Portugal and about 300 miles from the African coast. This uninhabited archipelago had been discovered in the early 1400s and colonized in 1425. Columbus married Doña Felipa Perestrello e Moniz, the daughter of the captain, or leader, of the island of Porto Santo. Their son Diego, who was to figure prominently in the early conquest of the New World, was born there about 1480.

The Azores, a chain of uninhabited islands strung out between 650 and 1,000 miles from the mainland, were discovered in the 1420s, although how and by whom is contested. The historian T. Bentley Duncan has unraveled the myth and early documentary record of the Azores in *Atlantic Islands*. An apparently well-informed cartographer put them on a map in 1439 and in the legend said, "These islands were found by Diego de Silues, pilot of the king of Portugal, in the year 1427." The islands were stocked with sheep by other Portuguese in the 1430s by order of Infante Dom Henrique (Prince Henry the

Navigator) and colonized about 1440 under the direction of Gonçalo Velho Cabral.

By 1450, the Azores were the most remote European outpost in the Atlantic. Getting there was a feat in itself. So if one wanted to sail west to the Far East, the islands seemed to offer a logical head start. One of the first to try this strategy was Fernão Dulmo, who lived in the group of the Azores called Terceira and had also heard Toscanelli's arguments. Dulmo's plan was to search first for Antilia, the semi-mythical "Island of the Seven Cities" that showed up on several maps as early as the late 1300s.

In the 1480s, Dulmo applied to the Portuguese king, Dom João II, for permission to sail west to look for Antilia. The Portuguese government contributed no money to the venture, and Dulmo demanded no specific rights and titles for lands he might find (making him a far cheaper alternative than Columbus, who asked for money, perpetual titles, shares in potential profits, and so on). Nevertheless, the king promised Dulmo suitable recompense, honors, and titles if he was successful.

Teaming up with João Estreito, a capable and ambitious sailor from the Madeiras, Dulmo sailed west from the Azores for forty days, longer than Columbus sailed on his first voyage to the New World. But because the Azores lie at a latitude where the westerlies blow, Dulmo sailed into the wind and into the Sargasso Sea, a vast floating morass of seaweed lying between the Azores and the Caribbean. After getting a long look at the middle of the Atlantic Ocean, he returned, having found nothing.

One of the maps that Dulmo used as a guide was drawn by a young German named Martin Behaim, an ambitious geographer and sailor who operated in the same circles as Dulmo, Estreito, and Columbus (they probably all knew each other personally, and certainly knew of each other). Behaim was a member of Portugal's Royal Maritime Commission—the committee that decided whom to sponsor on what voyages—and had already been knighted by the king. He too had a connection to the remote Atlantic islands, having married the daughter of the captain of the island of Fayal in the Azores. And he too had dreams of sailing west from the Azores.

Behaim had been trying for years to get the Portuguese king to give him ships and royal sponsorship. In 1493, after Columbus had returned from his first voyage but before anyone had heard the news,

Behaim had the most famous astronomer of his home city of Nuremberg write the Portuguese king and plead his case:

> You possess means and ample wealth; as also able mariners, eager to acquire immortality and fame. O what glory you would gain, if you made the habitable Orient known to the Occident, and what profits would its commerce give you, for you would make those islands of the Orient tributaries, and their kings amazed would quietly submit to your sovereignty! . . . And furthermore, our young man Martin Behaim is ready to take charge of such a voyage and set sail from the Azores whenever you say the word. (quoted in Morison 1942)

But Behaim's plans were overtaken by Columbus's discovery under Spain's flag. Columbus was the first to make it to the New World because—whether by luck or experience gained in his years at sea—he was the first to try the southern route. To go from the Azores westward, even though it was closer, was nearly impossible because of the winds. Columbus went far enough south that the easterly trade winds were in his favor and the north equatorial current carried him along.

These scenarios of ships, currents, wind patterns, and explorers' preconceptions fit into a larger context, however. After AD 1000 Europe had entered a phase of territorial expansion, similar to the expansion of the Muslims around AD 700 and the Romans in the first century BC. This accelerating expansion had motivated the Crusades and was driving the Portuguese down Africa's coastline. Europe's population was growing rapidly. The feudal system of the Middle Ages was dying while the Italian Renaissance was breaking new ground in artistic expression (witness the sculpture of Michelangelo [1475–1564] and the dome of Brunelleschi). The growing middle class had developed a taste for exotic goods from the East, but the Ottoman victory in Constantinople made the eastern route difficult. The best route to the East, as Toscanelli, Prince Henry, Dulmo, Estreito, Martin Behaim, and Columbus all believed, was to the West.

That Columbus had close competitors—the figures mentioned and others known and unknown—suggests that even if his voyage had ended in failure, the arrival of European ships on the eastern coasts of the Americas was inevitable. Would the past 500 years of culture contact have turned out differently if Fernão Dulmo had arrived first, landing on the coast of what is now Virginia? The possibilities for speculation are endless. For that matter, what would have happened if instead of landing in the Bahamas, Columbus had landed on Mexico's Gulf Coast and seen the Aztec empire at the height of its power? Columbus would have been more convinced than ever that he had reached the Orient. But he and his colleagues might well have been killed as threats to Aztec power, and the impact of Europe's expansion on the people of the New World would have been delayed for a few more years.

Works Cited and Suggestions for Further Reading

Columbus, Christopher
1893　　*The Journal of Christopher Columbus*. London: Hakluyt Society.

Dor-Ner, Zvi
1991　　*Columbus and the Age of Discovery*. New York: William Morrow and WGBH Educational Foundation.

Duncan, T. Bentley
1972　　*The Atlantic Islands*. Chicago and London: University of Chicago Press.

Morison, S. E.
1942　　*Admiral of the Ocean Sea*. New York: Little, Brown.

Sauer, Carl O.
1966　　*The Early Spanish Main*. Berkeley: University of California Press.

Wilson, Samuel M.
1990　　*Hispaniola: Caribbean Chiefdoms in the Age of Columbus*. Tuscaloosa: University of Alabama Press.

Columbus's Comeuppance

The Columbus of popular mythology died destitute and alone, unappreciated and unrewarded. In fact, he died a wealthy man, with his children at his bedside. Wherever he went in his last two years he was able to rent a nice house, full of servants. Near his chair he kept a small box of gold coins, which, had he been a different person, might have served to remind him that he had done pretty well for having been born a Genoese weaver's son. Instead, it acted as a painful reminder of all the things he thought he was owed and all that had been taken from him.

Before his first voyage, Columbus had been summoned to the royal camp at Santa Fé, from which King Ferdinand and Queen Isabela were directing the siege of Grenada, the last Moorish stronghold in Spain. There Columbus was granted permission to set out across the Atlantic, and with representatives of the Crown, he drew up a document called the Capitulaciónes (agreements) of Santa Fé. Even in the fifteenth century, lawyers managed to make legal documents overly long, yet obscure, but this agreement clearly contained a number of items that offered Columbus and his heirs great rewards. Juan de Coloma, a senior official of the Spanish court, negotiated the terms and notarized each agreement for the king and queen (and probably regretted it later). The first two parts dealt with Columbus's title of Admiral of the Ocean Sea and his titles on any land he might find, viceroy and governor general:

> Your Highnesses appoint Don Cristóbal Colón to be your Admiral in all those islands and mainlands which by his activity and industry shall be

discovered or acquired in the Ocean Sea, during his lifetime, and likewise, after his death, his heirs and successors one after another in perpetuity. . . . Likewise, that Your Highnesses appoint the said Don Cristóbal Colón to be your Viceroy and Governor General in all the said islands and mainlands.

The third part dealt with Columbus's share of the profits:

Item, that of all and every kind of merchandise, whether pearls, precious stones, gold, silver, spices, and other objects and merchandise whatsoever, of whatever kind, name and sort, which may be bought, bartered, discovered, acquired and obtained within the limits of the said Admiralty, Your Highnesses grant from now henceforth to the said Don Cristóbal, and will that he may have and take for himself, the tenth part of the whole, after deducting all the expenses which may be incurred therein, so that of what part shall remain clear and free he may have and take the tenth part for himself, and may do therewith as he pleases, the other nine parts being reserved for Your Highnesses.

The fourth part dealt with protecting Columbus from lawsuits, and the fifth stated that "the said Don Cristóbal Colón may, if he chooses, contribute and pay the eighth part of all that may be spent in the equipment [of voyages by others], and that likewise he may have and take the eighth part of the profits that may result from such equipment.—It so pleases their Highnesses. Juan de Coloma" (translated in Wilford 1991).

Columbus lost most of the concessions named in the Capitulaciónes between their signing on April 17, 1492, and his death fourteen years later. The discovery of gold-producing islands and the ever-increasing prospects of other undiscovered territories in the Americas outweighed both legal and moral restraints (certainly little of either was shown the people who had lived in these lands for ten millennia).

One by one Columbus's claims to the wealth being taken from the Americas slipped away. The "tenth" of everything soon became a tenth of the Crown's "royal fifth"—in other words 2 percent rather than 10 percent (still a fortune). The "eighth," his legitimate part of the profits of any voyage that he invested in, was very slow to arrive, if it ever did. As Columbus's health failed and he lost favor with the king, his partners in these voyages stalled on their payments.

Columbus also lost the titles of viceroy and governor general after proving himself a disaster as a leader. Columbus used people as tools, bullied and cheated them, and from the first voyage there was no shortage of people who hated him. Columbus even went back on his promise to give a decent lifelong pension to the first sailor who saw land on the first voyage: In the early morning of October 12, 1492, Rodrigo de Triana saw the island of San Salvador (Guanahani), but once it became clear that it was land, Columbus remembered that in fact he had seen land some hours before.

Even Columbus's supporter, the priest and historian Bartolomé de Las Casas, had to concede that the Columbus family, and the Admiral of the Ocean Sea in particular, "did not show modesty and discretion in governing Spaniards which they should have done." A foreigner— not even an aristocratic foreigner—treated Spanish gentlemen as if they were servants. Columbus's brief reign as leader of the Spanish forces in the Indies was marked by mutiny and rebellion. What he did to the indigenous people he met in the New World was even worse.

In 1500, under orders from the Crown, Francisco de Bobadilla sailed to Hispaniola, took over the government, and arrested Columbus (then on his third voyage). Columbus was put in irons and sent back to Spain. As far as the Spanish government was concerned, this took care of his claim to being viceroy and governor general of the Indies. The Genoese Columbus had once again become a foreigner in the land. Although he and his descendants continued to battle in the courts, they had little legal recourse against the Crown.

Columbus was not yet out of business, however. Between 1500 and 1502 he deluged the court, mostly the queen, with letters concerning a long-held obsession of his—capturing Jerusalem and the sepulcher of Christ, then under Islamic control. The historian Felipe Fernández-Armesto, in his splendid book *Columbus* (1991), finds that Columbus gave three arguments supporting his dream: First, the Holy Spirit had told him to do it, and in support of this he cited the many ways in which he had been given divine help in the past; second, success would be certain if the king and queen and their subjects had faith in God (and, Columbus believed, they did); and, finally, both scriptural prophecies and astrological predictions—"signs in the heavens"— indicated that victory was certain. As Fernández-Armesto points out, these prophecies and predictions had to do with the coming end of the world, a prospect that haunted Columbus.

Engraving of Columbus, by Theodor de Bry, 1595 (from Icones Quinquaginta Virorum, *Frankfurt, 1597).*

Largely to get rid of Columbus, hoping that at last he would perish at sea, Ferdinand and Isabela gave him leave to make one more trip to the Indies. Columbus set out with four small ships. Financing was easy to come by in this period of great promise, but he put up some of his own money for the venture. The king and queen expressly forbade him to go to Hispaniola (except perhaps for a stop on the way back), but completely in character, he headed there first.

When he reached Santo Domingo, Spain's principal port in the Indies, Columbus was refused anchorage, so he stayed at sea off the southern coast of Hispaniola while he tried to negotiate with the city's commander. Soon Columbus began to observe changes in the winds, clouds, and tides that were like those he had seen in previous brushes with hurricanes. He prepared his ships for the storm and sent word to Santo Domingo advising captains not to leave port. Despite Columbus's warning, a treasure fleet of about twenty-six vessels set sail for Spain. Columbus's four ships managed to survive the hurricane intact, but the treasure fleet lost twenty ships and more than 500 men, among them Bobadilla and the courageous Taíno chief Guarionex (see "Columbus, My Enemy," this volume).

Columbus then toured the coast of Central America, where he had to abandon two of his ships. They had been turned into unseaworthy sponges by the borers that feasted on their wood hulls. The other two ships, the *Capitana* and the *Santiago*, were nearly as bad off. They barely made it to Jamaica, and on June 25, 1503, just before they sank, Columbus had them run onto a sandbar in Saint Ann's Bay. The hulks were roped together and turned into swampy living quarters for the disgusted and demoralized crew.

On July 7, 1503, more than ten years after he had landed in the Caribbean for the first time, Columbus wrote to the Spanish king and queen:

> I came to serve Your Highnesses at the age of twenty-eight, and now I have no hair upon me that is not white, and my body is infirm and exhausted. All that was left to me and to my brothers has been taken away and sold, even to the cloak that I wore, to my great dishonor. . . . Until now, I have wept for others; now may the skies have pity on me, and may the earth weep for me. Of things material I have not even a penny to give the Church; in things spiritual, here in the Indies, I have been separated from any form of Catholic life. Isolated in this pain, sick, expecting death every day, surrounded by a host of cruel savages and our enemies, and thus separated from the holy sacraments of holy Church, how neglected will be this soul if here it parts from my body. Weep for me, whoever has charity, truth and justice. I did not come on this voyage to navigate for gain, honor or wealth; this is certain, for any hope I had of such things is dead. I came to Your Highnesses with honest purpose and sincere zeal, and I do not lie. I humbly beg your Highnesses that, if God sees fit to remove me from this place, you will aid me to go to Rome and on other pilgrimages. You whose lives and high state the Sacred Trinity guards and increases.

Half the company mutinied after a few months and wandered the northeastern coast of Jamaica, preying on the Taíno Indians who lived

there. Columbus sent Diego Méndez de Salcedo to Hispaniola in a
Taíno canoe with hired paddlers to get a ship to rescue him, but it was
nearly a year in coming. Columbus and his crew (including those who
had mutinied) then jammed themselves into the decrepit ship,
smaller than any of the four caravels they had begun the voyage with,
and somehow made it back to Hispaniola and then to Spain.

The disastrous fourth voyage ruined any chance Columbus had of
ever returning to the Indies or of ever regaining his title of viceroy. It
demonstrated that he was washed up as an explorer and agent of the
king, and it finished the job of wrecking his health. The king and
queen were probably not thrilled to see Columbus return. The queen,
who at many critical points had supported Columbus, was gravely ill
and died less than a month after his return. Columbus had been
stripped of all of his titles except that of admiral, and he was in poor
health and increasingly desperate. In every letter to the king he included the same refrain: "Where is my tenth, my eighth, my third?"
The "third" in this litany was a strange figment of his imagination
and a symptom of his increasingly irrational state of mind. Earlier ad-
mirals of Spain's then-small island domains in the Mediterranean,
having paid for the colonization and development of the islands
themselves, had kept a third of all profits, much the way a feudal lord
got a large cut of his estate's produce.

In his mind, Columbus twisted this inapplicable precedent to
mean that he should get a third of the proceeds of the Indies—not
the 2 percent he in fact received, or the 10 percent he demanded, or
the 20 percent the Spanish government got, but 33 percent for himself and his descendants forevermore. For months on end the king ig-
nored Columbus, not answering his letters or asking him to visit the
court. This was an exquisite form of torture for a person like Columbus, who hated to wait for anything but had spent his whole life in
excruciating delays, broken by brief and usually calamitous flurries of
activity. Before his first voyage the king had kept him sitting and
waiting for ten years for a license to sail west, turning the matter over
to committee after committee or otherwise putting Columbus on
hold. When Columbus was deposed as viceroy of Hispaniola in 1500
and sent back to Spain in chains (he refused the captain's offer to remove them), the king and queen had let him sit (still in chains) for
six weeks after his arrival in Spain.

Of all the periods of inactivity he was forced to endure, this final
one was the most agonizing of all, because Columbus, King Ferdi-

nand, and everyone else knew that Columbus did not have many months to live. Soon, Columbus knew, his arthritic and gout-ridden body would fail him, and it would be too late. And Ferdinand knew that soon he would be rid of this annoying foreigner forever, this lowly born and overly successful pest whom he had come to genuinely loathe over the years.

Columbus sought comfort from his children, whom he manipulated and used but certainly seemed to love. Some of his last letters to Diego, his eldest son and heir (born to his wife, Doña Felipa Perestrello e Moniz, who had died young), contain moving pleas for the respect or at least love of his child. These letters all began, "My very dear son," and ended "Your father, who loves you more than himself." The relationship of Columbus and Diego was troubled, however, because Diego had what Columbus wanted most—the ear of the king. Diego had been in the queen's guard at court, and after her death in 1504, he had become part of the king's inner circle. So these letters between Columbus and Diego are torn by the admiral's love for his son and his urgent wish that Diego press his compulsive and unrealistic demands on the king.

Columbus's letter of December 1, 1504, following another written three days earlier, begins: "My very dear Son: After I received your letter of November 15th, nothing more has been heard from you. I wish you would send me some small message. Every hour I hope to receive a letter from you." He rambles on about financial problems, asking for information about the king's state of mind on this and that matter, mentioning again "the third and the tenth," and complaining that he had "not received the tenth, except the tenth of what Their Highnesses receive." At the end he reminds his son to write, adding, as subtly as an unsubtle man was able, a hint suggesting that Diego could send word if he wanted to: "Every day messengers from where you are arrive here." The letter closes: "Our Lord help you in your sacred duty. Done in Seville on the 1st of December. Your father who loves you more than himself."

Columbus signed, as always with his formal signature, a cryptic stack of letters that he asked his heirs to use as their own but never really explained.

Although his meaning for the first three lines probably will never be precisely known, the historian Samuel Eliot Morison believes the simplest answer is that they correspond to the Latin formula *Servus Sum Altissimi Salvatoris*—"Servant I am of the Highest Saviour"—with the third line representing Christ, Mary, and Jesus, or perhaps Joseph. But the signature may be read up and down as well as across, and according to some scholars, it contains complex references to the North Star, Santiago, the Christian cross, and a ship's mast. The last line in the signature expresses the view Columbus promoted of himself in his last letter: *Xpo* is a Greeklike rendition of Cristóbal and also Christ, and *FERENS* means "carrier," referring to the Christ bearer. Columbus thought he was destined to expand Christendom, chosen specifically by God to do what he had done. In his last months he sometimes slipped and spoke of the New World as he conceived of it—"the Indies, which God has given to me."

As Columbus neared death, he tried to stop his pathetic and ineffectual struggling. He wrote to Diego de Garza, a sometimes-sympathetic friend and eventually the archbishop of Seville, saying,

> Since it appears that His Highness does not intend to comply with the promise he made me by his spoken word and in writing, together with the Queen who now is in heaven, I think that my carrying on this fight, being only a simple laborer, would be like sailing into the wind; it would be well for me to leave this to God our Lord. He has always helped me and looked after my needs.

Death, his destiny, and the deeds of his enemies preoccupied Columbus. In his notes, he wrote down biblical prophecies and connections of his experiences with lists of biblical passages, and in the margin wrote a long and complex poem. The poem was in Spanish but at the beginning of each verse was a Latin phrase; when the Latin phrases from the six verses are combined they spell out a message: "Be mindful of thy most recent actions and thou shalt avoid sin in eternity." The last verse of Columbus's poem, in the artful translation of Felipe Fernández-Armesto, reads:

> *Sinless be, and contemplate*
> *The agonies of those who die,*
> *How grief and terror are the fate*
> *Of sinners in their wretched state.*
> *Think well, as far as in thee lie,*
> *Upon the just, released at last*
> *From travails suffered in the past,*
> *Into the light eternally.*

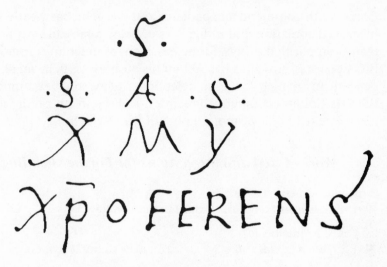

Columbus's signature, from his correspondence.

On March 20, 1506, at the age of fifty-five, Columbus died. Around him were his sons, Diego and Fernando; his brothers, Bartolomé and Diego; and a few servants and supporters. His last words are said to have been "In manus tuas, Domine, commendo spiritum meum" (Into your hands, Lord, I commend my spirit)—but deathbed scenes are never quite so sanitary and romantic as those writing later make them out to be.

What gold Columbus had accumulated dissipated in two genera-tions. (Although Columbus's eldest son Diego married extremely well and linked the Columbus name with an established and powerful aristocratic lineage that endured, his son Luís traded any claim to the profits from the New World for a much smaller title and fiefdom than those Columbus was offered, and then he squandered them.) The grandiose promises that the king and queen of Spain drew up be-fore his first voyage with such an unlikely prospect as the Italian Cristoforo Colombo were one by one bought off or nullified in the interest of national security. The Crown wrote this awkward associa-tion off to experience and never made the same mistake again.

Today, Cristóbal Colón, the linear descendant of the sailor who ran into the West Indies on the way to the East Indies and never knew the difference, is a lieutenant commander in the Spanish Navy Air

Corps. With commendable patience and grace, he has weathered the misplaced adulation and indignities of being a tangible symbol of so many complicated things, for he has about as much in common with his ancestor as any of us has. Yet on his business card, in small letters, beneath his name, above his telephone, telex, and fax numbers, is the title Columbus fought the hardest to keep in his family forever: Almirante del Mar Océano, Admiral of the Ocean Sea.

Works Cited and Suggestions for Further Reading

Fernández-Armesto, Felipe
1991   *Columbus*. New York: Oxford University Press.

Las Casas, Bartolomé de
1951   *Historia de las Indias*. Mexico: Fondo de Cultural Económica.

Morison, Samuel Eliot
1991 [1942]   *Admiral of the Ocean Sea: A Life of Christopher Columbus.*
               Little, Brown (reprint edition).

Todorov, Tzvetan
1984   *The Conquest of America: The Question of the Other.* New York: Harper
         & Row.

Wilford, John Noble.
1991   *The Mysterious History of Columbus: An Exploration of the Man, the
         Myth, the Legacy.* New York: Knopf.

Contrast

and

Coincidence in the Americas

T he first chapters in this section explore some of the remarkable similarities between societies of the Americas and the Old World. These two great branches of humanity, separated for so long, proceeded along remarkably similar paths. Each developed agriculture, urbanism, and all the complex accouterments of high civilization. Cortés and his small army went into an Aztec capital that was laid out very much like European cities of the day, and the lives of urban dwellers in both places were similar, right down to the tax burden they carried.

In "White Legends and Lost Tribes," I look at a further similarity: In their first encounters, both Native Americans and Europeans sought to understand the other by reference to their own history and mythology. Europeans looked for the origins of the American people in the Lost Tribes of Israel or Atlantis or other loose ends in history. The people of the Americas did the same, searching for clues as to how these others might be expected to behave.

From our perspective, these identifications can be seen as illusory—stories told about the past that make sense in a particular cultural context. This is part of the nature of history, however. It is perhaps impossible to isolate the objective truth about past events (although some versions are clearly closer than others). In two of the chapters in this section, "'That Unmanned, Wild Countrey'" and "Pilgrim's Paradox," I explore the ways that narratives about the past can rewrite history in ways favorable to the tellers.

The chapters in this section also explore some specific cases in which chance played a crucial role in the course of events. In "Pandora's Bite," I look at the impact of epidemic disease on both the native peoples of the Americas and the Europeans. In "The Matter of Smallpox," I try to capture some of the horror of such an awful and powerful disease over the last 500 years. The events of the past centuries have brought people from all over the world together in the same place, in the Americas and elsewhere. But all of the diseases that evolved in relative isolation have also been brought together. Large-scale epidemics have always accompanied episodes of increased contact, and the results of the present contact period are very likely not over.

White Legends
and Lost Tribes

I n the last years of his reign, the Aztec emperor Montezuma received this omen:

> Certain Fishermen near the Lake of Mexico took a monstrous Fowl, of extraordinary Make and Bigness; and accounting it valuable for its Novelty, presented the same to the King. Its Deformity was horrible; and on the Head of it was a shining Plate like a Looking-Glass, from which the Sun reflected a sort of dim and melancholy Light. Montezuma observed it, and drawing nearer to take a better View, saw within it a Representation of the Night, amidst whose Obscurity were seen some Parts of the Heaven covered with Stars, and so distinctly represented, that he turned his Eyes to the sun, as one doubtful of the Day: And upon fixing his Eyes the second Time on that seeming Glass, he spy'd, instead of Night, what gave him greater Astonishment; for there appeared to his Sight an Army of Men, that came from the East, making a terrible Slaughter of his Subjects. He assembled the Magicians and Priests to consult about this Prodigy, and the Bird stood immoveable, till many of them had tried the same Experiment—but then it got away, and vanish'd in their Presence, leaving them another Presage in its astonishing Flight. (Solis y Rivandeneyra 1973)

When Cortés and his small army of Spaniards set about conquering Mexico, the relevance of this powerful omen suddenly appeared obvious. Initially, however, Montezuma thought Cortés to be the earthly manifestation of the god Quetzalcoatl, returning to Mexico. According to legend, Quetzalcoatl had gone by sea to join the Sun god, leaving word he would return; all Montezuma's predecessors had expected him. It seemed impossible that Cortés could be anyone else.

Montezuma sent emissaries from Tenochtitlán, the Aztec capital, to meet Cortés, bearing the clothes and adornments Quetzalcoatl would need: "Our god and our lord, be very welcomed, for we, your servants and vassals, have been waiting for you a very long time. Your vassal and lieutenant of your kingdom, Montezuma, has sent us to greet and receive you. He says that our lord and god should be very welcome, and here we bring all the precious adornments that you used among us as our king and god."

Forewarned, Cortés played along in order to gain an advantage over the Aztecs. Their confidence in his identity steadily eroded, however. As Cortés drew closer to Tenochtitlán, attracting allies from the Indian groups opposed to Aztec rule, Montezuma's advisers warned against letting such a dangerous person into the capital.

When Cortés arrived at the temple of Quetzalcoatl, for what some still believed would be the resumption of the god's role, he showed himself to be an enemy of the ancient god.

In a sense, Montezuma had known the conquering strangers all his life. They bore a remarkable resemblance to some of the extraordinary creatures that inhabited the Aztecs' elaborate legends and myths. The critical narratives, and their correct interpretations, became apparent as events unfolded.

Similar premonitions of the coming of white strangers are noted in nearly all chronicles of encounters between people of the New World and the Old. They constitute a special class of folklore, because those who recorded them also starred in them. They are premonitions recorded after the fact, which makes accurate prediction seem easy. But the stories cannot be discounted as postcontact inventions; they are deeply woven into the fabric of Native American folk traditions, with modified versions of the same stories found in groups thousands of miles apart.

Stories of bearded men in clothes or of people who might, in a postconquest light, fit the description of Europeans were told in the eastern woodlands and on the plains of North America. In the Southwest, the Hopi ritual calendar counted off the years before the predicted return of Panáha, the lost white brother. Among the Taíno of

Hispaniola, the first New World inhabitants encountered by Columbus, sacred songs recounted their history and the exploits of their ancestors. They included love tales, heroic epics, stories of the origins of the Taíno, and predictions of their demise.

One Taíno song, which was set down by Pietro Martire d'Anghera, stated, "Magnacochios [clothed men] shall disembark in the island, armed with swords and with one stroke cut a man in two, and our descendants shall bend beneath their yoke." Francisco López de Gómara recorded another version of the same song: "Before many years passed some men would come with long beards and clothing all over their bodies; they would trample the ancient gods of the land and forbid the traditional rites, and they would spill the blood of the Taíno's offspring and make them slaves."

The rulers of the Inca empire had also experienced visions of the arrival of clothed and bearded men. One Inca ruler of the late fourteenth and early fifteenth centuries called himself Viracocha, after the god he saw in his revelation. He had a temple built to commemorate his dream and, dressing himself as a model of the person in his vision, had a statue carved to represent it. According to Garcilaso de la Vega,

> The image was of a man of good height with a beard more than a span in length: he wore a long loose garment like a tunic or cassock, reaching to his feet. He held a strange animal of unknown shape with claws like a lion's and with a chain round its neck and the end of it in the statue's hand.

As with Cortés and Montezuma, the identification of the Spaniards with Viracocha's vision played to the Europeans' advantage:

> As the prince said that it had a beard, unlike the Indians who are usually without hair on the face, and that it was dressed from head to foot while the Indians are clad differently and their dress does not go below the knees, the word Viracocha was duly applied to the first Spaniards who entered Peru, who were seen to be bearded and dressed from head to foot. Because they regarded the Spaniards as the children of their god, they respected them so much that they worshiped them and scarcely defended themselves against them.

While the Native Americans interpreted the arrival of the Europeans as confirmation of their legends and omens, the Europeans

Illustration of an encomendero and Andean people,
by Guaman Poma de Ayala, from Historia Gráfica
del Perú, *1613*

saw these same traditions as containing a true reflection of events.
The ubiquitous legends of white men and women were taken as evidence of earlier contacts with the Old World or of Old World
prophets visiting the New World. Rarely, if ever, were they seen for
what they were: People's attempts to make sense of inexplicable
events by looking to and reinterpreting some aspects of their historical or mythic past.

Just as the Native Americans sought to comprehend the foreign in-
truders, the Europeans searched their own histories and legends for

accounts of groups fitting the description of the New World people, so that they could better understand them.

Columbus, who clung until his death to the belief that he had found a shorter route to the East Indies that Marco Polo and others had described, simply called the Native Americans "Indians," a misnomer that persists to this day.

In the early 1500s, most Europeans had little acquaintance with the Far East and sought explanations closer to home. Classical scholars provided some intriguing possibilities. A story of a Carthaginian voyage to a large and fertile island across the Atlantic, attributed to a work by Aristotle (*Mirabilibus aut Seculationibus*), seemed to many to account for the peopling of the New World. Others, such as Pietro Martire d'Anghera, took their cue from the Bible, suggesting that a fleet sent westward by Solomon had probably visited Hispaniola.

Gonzalo Fernández de Oviedo y Valdéz introduced an opportune legalistic twist (in an arena of competing European claims over rights to exploit the New World) when he wrote that the people of the New World might be of Spanish descent. He cited the highly questionable chronicler Berosus, who said that Héspero, the twelfth King of Spain (whose rule was said to have begun about 1658 BC), had sent a fleet westward. According to Oviedo, they planted a Spanish flag, preceding any other European claim by three millennia.

For Europeans of the time, Atlantis—the vast mid-Atlantic continent whose advanced civilization and catastrophic destruction were described by Plato—was a semimythical, semihistorical place. Many writers speculated that some of Atlantis's population had escaped to the west as the island sank beneath the waves. Perhaps the first to suggest this was Francisco López de Gómara, secretary to, and champion of, Cortés, who despised and vilified New World Indians and in his writings kept their origins as far offshore as possible. Others, probably independently, came to the same conclusion.

In general, the prime candidates in the sixteenth-century search for the origins of the New World peoples were the historical or mythical loose ends in the Western tradition: Explorers who had not returned, protagonists of classical works who had dropped from sight, and so on were all suspects. The ten lost tribes of Israel also fit into this category, although explanations invoking them as the source of New World populations did not really gain popularity until the eighteenth and nineteenth centuries. Columbus thought Hispaniola may have been the island of Ophir mentioned in I Kings, whereas Diego de Landa, in his *Account of the Affairs of Yucatan,* noted that some of the old people of Yucatan claim to have heard from their ancestors that this land was settled by people from the east whom god had liberated by cutting twelve paths for them through the sea. If this were true, it must be that all the inhabitants of the Indies are descended from the Jews.

Nevertheless, despite this tendency to search for ready-made explanations, some early writers came fairly close to the view that modern scholars hold, that New World peoples came from northeast Asia. Amerigo Vespucci, in a 1506 letter, compared the Indians to people from eastern Asia: "They have broad faces, so that their appearance may be that of the Tartar." A Portuguese trader named Antonio Galvão had spent time in the Orient on the Portuguese island of Ternate in the Moluccas and there heard a claim that Chinese sailors had discovered the New World. He observed that both the Chinese and Native Americans had similar "fashions and customs" and that they both had "small eies [and] flat noses." Another Portuguese, Pero de Magalhães, also saw similarities in facial structure between the Indians of Brazil and the Chinese.

The complex realities of the similarities and differences between human groups in the New and Old Worlds, so long separated, defied simple interpretation. Bartolomé de Las Casas, who had extensive firsthand experience with Native American cultures in several regions, cautioned against making claims about the origins of New World peoples on the basis of a few coincidences. For example, he argued against regarding the isolated practice of circumcision among Yucatecan Indians as evidence of a Jewish origin. Las Casas's detailed descriptions and analyses of Native American cultures spoke against such facile assertions. And as a result of what must have been the first New World archeological excavation, carried out in the early 1500s, Las Casas recognized the great antiquity of the New World people:

> I have seen in these mines of Cibao [on Hispaniola], one or two yards deep in the virgin earth, in the plains at the foot of some hills, burned wood and ashes as if a few days past a fire had been made there. And for the same reason we have to conclude that in other times the river came near there, and in such a place they made a fire, and afterwards the river moved farther away. Soil accumulated there, as the rains brought it down from the hills, and covered the site. And because this could not

happen except by the passage of many years and most ancient time, there is therefore a strong argument that the people of these islands and the mainland are very ancient.

Works Cited and Suggestions for Further Reading

Landa, Diego de
1975   *The Maya: Diego de Landa's Account of the Affairs of Yucatan.* Edited and translated by A. R. Pagden. Chicago: J. P. O'Hara.

Las Casas, Bartolomé de
1951   *Historia de las Indias.* Mexico: Fondo de Cultural Económica.

Martire de Anghiera, Pietro
1970 [1912]   *De Orbe Novo, the Eight Decades of Peter Martyr d'Anghera.* Translated from the Latin with notes and introduction by Francis Augustus MacNutt. New York: Burt Franklin.

Solis y Rivandeneyra, Antonio de
1973 [1753]   *The History of the Conquest of Mexico by the Spaniards.* New York: AMS Press.

Vega, Garcilaso de la
1966   *Royal Commentaries of the Incas, and General History of Peru.* Translated with an introduction by Harold V. Livermore. Foreword by Arnold J. Toynbee. Austin: University of Texas Press.

The Gardeners of Eden

G ardens and gardening flourished during the Italian Renaissance, reflecting both the rebirth of interest in classical phi-
losophy and aesthetics and the emergence of the natural sciences. The remarkable *Natural History* written by Pliny the Elder (AD
23–79) was resurrected as holy writ by Renaissance gardeners. Pliny's
principles are still adhered to in modern gardens, especially his em-
phasis on integrating the rooms of the villa with the "rooms" of the
garden and the importance of maintaining harmony between the
villa garden and the surrounding landscape.

The villa at Careggi was just one of the country estates that the
Medici family of Florence owned in the late 1400s, but its Renaissance garden was Lorenzo de' Medici's favorite. He spared no expense
in researching and obtaining the most exotic plants for it: A fifteenth-century poem by Alexander Bracci lists more than 100 species
that Lorenzo planted. Leonardo da Vinci, who lived from 1452 to
1519, spent considerable time at Careggi, creating sculpture and perhaps even designing parts of his patron's cherished garden. As the
botanist William Emboden has shown, Leonardo was as passionate a
student of botany as he was of nearly everything else in his world.
His voluminous notebooks contain thousands of detailed sketches of
plants, with notes on their characteristics (set down in his mirror-
image handwriting), as well as sketches of gardens.

More than four centuries later, in another country, I too keep a garden. Mine is certainly not impressive by any measure, even compared with the gardens on our street. But my international hodgepodge of plants would have thrilled Lorenzo de' Medici, Leonardo da Vinci, and Pliny the Elder. The plants are unremarkable and commonplace in many gardens, but in addition to many local natives such as coneflowers and coreopsis, there are plants that were domesticated in Asia, Africa, Central and South America, and Europe.

Leonardo never saw the explosion of New World plants into the gardens of Europe and the rest of the world. He mentions only one or two Native American plants in his notebooks—corn (maize) and possibly a New World bean. He died just as Cortés's expedition was making its way toward the Aztec capital and some of the world's most remarkable gardens. So Leonardo never tasted chocolate, one of the things Cortés brought to Europe.

Describing the extraordinary things Cortés and his army saw in Montezuma's palaces, Bernal Diaz del Castillo wrote, in *The Discovery and Conquest of Mexico:*

> We must not forget the gardens of flowers and sweet-scented trees, and the many kinds that there were of them, and the arrangement of them and the walks, and the ponds; and tanks of fresh water where the water entered at one end and flowed out of the other; and the baths which he had there, and the variety of small birds that nested in the branches, and the medicinal and useful herbs that were in the gardens. It was a wonder to see, and to take care of it there were many gardeners.

The sixteenth-century chronicler Fernando de Alva Ixtilxochitl was born to a noble Aztec family but educated in Spanish mission schools. In his *Historia Chichimeca* he described the precinct of the Aztec aristocracy as a huge walled park, containing palaces, temples, and the buildings of the state bureaucracy. The rest of the precinct was given over to gardens,

> with many fountains, ponds and canals, many fish and birds, and the whole planted with more than two thousand pines . . . and there were several mazes, according to where the king bathed; and once a man was in he could not find the way out . . . and farther on, beside the temples, there was the bird-house, where the king kept all the kinds and varieties of birds, animals, reptiles and serpents that they brought him from every part of New Spain; and those which were not to be had were rep-

Page from Leonardo da Vinci's notebook showing illustration of a flower, with discussion in his mirror-image script. (Courtesy of the Benson Latin American Collection)

resented in gold and precious stones—which was also the case with the fish, both those of the sea and those that lived in rivers and lakes. So no bird, fish or animal of the whole country was wanting here: they were there either alive or figured in gold and gems.

In the 1570s, Francisco Hernández and a group of Aztec artists made a large compendium of Aztec plants. Unfortunately, the original drawings, containing additional notations and details in the Aztec language, Nahuatl, were destroyed in 1671 with a large part of the famous library at El Escorial, a Spanish palace and monastery. But copies of them appear in *Historia Naturae Maxime Peregrinae* (1635), by the Jesuit Juan Eusebio Niremberg.

Another source describing the Aztec flora is the 1552 Badianus Manuscript. This extraordinary catalog of medicinal plants, with still-vivid, natural-dye illustrations, was made by two Aztec scholars educated at the Colegio de Santa Cruz de Tlatelolco. Martinus de la Cruz composed the text, and Juannes Badianus translated it into Latin. The book sat in the Vatican library for nearly four centuries before its facsimile was published in 1940.

Many of the New World's most spectacular contributions to modern gardens were slow to appear in Europe. The conquerors paid more attention to crops that could be profitably sold. Two of the most addictive, and thus most profitable, were cacao (the source of chocolate) and tobacco. Tomatoes were slower to catch on in Europe, only becoming widely grown in the late nineteenth century. Potatoes, squashes, pumpkins, arrowroot, manioc, and other food plants were not addicting but became popular and important in many parts of the world. Some Native American crops, like the peanut, have come into their own only in the last century or so. And some, like the wonderful Jerusalem artichoke, a member of the sunflower family, have not yet become popular but should (its intriguing name is a corruption of the Italian *girasole,* meaning "turn to the sun").

The chili pepper (*Capsicum annuum* and others) well illustrates the massive diffusion of plants that has taken place since 1492. In his journal of the first voyage, Columbus noted, "There is also much chili, which is their pepper, of a kind more valuable than [black] pepper, and none of the people eat without it, for they find it very healthful. Fifty caravels can be loaded with it each year in Hispaniola."

This remarkable plant—domesticated, bred into dozens of varieties, and cultivated in the New World for thousands of years—made its way around the globe in just a few decades. The spicy cuisines of South Asia, Thailand, Vietnam, and Sichuan in China are unimaginable without chili.

Scholars have often noted the dramatic effect of the exchange of New and Old World food plants—including corn, potatoes, and tomatoes going one way and wheat, rice, and bananas going the other. In sheer numbers of species, however, the relocation of ornamental plants has been vastly greater than the movements of economically important species. Ironically, many domesticated and well-bred New World ornamental plants, left to fend for themselves when their gardeners died or left their gardens, were rediscovered by Europeans as "wild" flowers.

The twelve species of dahlias grown by the Aztecs were warmly received in Europe, but they did not reach England until 1790. The zinnias and marigolds were probably grown earlier in Spain and other

Mediterranean countries but were first recorded in England in 1753. The glorious lilies of the Andean Incan gardeners, such as the hardy amaryllis, the Peruvian lily, and rain lilies, are widely cultivated today. Both Incan and Aztec gardeners grew many varieties of bromeliads (relatives of the pineapple, another New World domesticate), whose vast family spreads over all the tropical Americas.

Others among the countless New World flowers in global cultivation are phlox, morning glory, fuchsias, Michaelmas daisies, and yuccas. Anyone who gardens is probably growing New World domesticates, including those who dedicate all their efforts to trying to grow the elusive 1,000-pound pumpkin. Thousands of wildflowers are also finding increasing popularity among gardeners. Just a few of the sophisticated native plants I have growing in my garden are the primrose, Mexican mint marigold, butterfly weed, black-eyed Susan, and hairy zexmenia.

Such wild plants are the raw material for gardeners. With food crops, cultivators can select for edible wild plants that yield more food per plant, are better suited to particular conditions, are more hardy, and so forth. Gardeners select blooms and foliage for size, form, texture, and color. Five hundred years ago, the New World, Asia, and Africa were full of raw material for plant domestication, whereas Europe had relatively little. In *The Principles of Gardening*, Hugh Johnson argues that the flora of Europe suffered much greater damage during the last glaciation than did that of Asia and the Americas. In North America and China, plant communities survived by migrating southward as the glaciers crept forward, and they recolonized as the glaciers retreated. European plants were cut off by the Mediterranean Sea, and only the most hardy survived.

Europe's colonial expansion changed that situation, and European gardens began to fill with the exotic flowers of Africa; Asia; and, eventually, the Americas. The rose represents a delightful combination of the musk rose of the Mediterranean and Near East and the Chinese rose, neither of which in its wild form is as glorious as the hybrid offspring. The Renaissance painter Botticelli sprinkled some of the early hybrid roses around in the background of *The Birth of Venus*. We have seen only a few centuries of the combination and recombination of the lesser-known species in the world's flora, and other startling hybrids have yet to appear.

Europe's expansion was driven by a growing population and an even faster growing aristocracy, which generated a demand for gold, spices, and other rare and exotic goods. Columbus sailed west to find a quicker route to these luxuries, a good shipload of which—safely delivered—could allow a captain to retire for life. Although they might seem secondary in importance to economic crops, exotic or ornamental plants, destined to grace the celebrated gardens of the Renaissance aristocracy, were valued for their aesthetic properties. Just as I can imagine an Aztec king conquering whole provinces to obtain the twelfth dahlia, I am confident Lorenzo de' Medici would have been willing to pay more than the total cost of Columbus's first voyage to get a few more specimens for his garden at Careggi.

Works Cited and Suggestions for Further Reading

Cruz, Martín de la
1940 [1552]   *The Badianus Manuscript: An Aztec Herbal of 1552.* Balti
                more: Johns Hopkins University Press.

Diaz del Castillo, Bernal
1963   *The Discovery and Conquest of Mexico.* New York: Viking Press.

Emboden, William
1987   *Leonardo da Vinci on Plants and Gardens.* Portland, OR: Dioscorides
         Press.

Ixtilxochitl, Fernando de Alva
         Historia Chichimeca. Mexico: Vargas Rea.

Johnson, Hugh
1997   *The Principles of Gardening: The Practice of the Gardener's Art.* New
         York: Simon & Schuster.

Niremberg, Juan Eusebio
1635   *Historia Naturae Maxime Peregrinae.* Antwerp: Plantiniana B. Moreti.

Pliny the Elder
1991   *Natural History: A Selection by the Elder Pliny.* Excerpted and trans-
         lated by John F. Healey. New York: Penguin USA.

Soustelle, Jacques
1961   *Daily Life of the Aztecs.* Stanford: Stanford University Press.

Thacker, Christopher
1985   *The History of Gardens.* Berkeley: University of California Press.

Viola, Herman J., and Carolyn Margolis (eds.)
1991   *Seeds of Change: A Quincentennial Commemoration.* Washington, DC:
         Smithsonian Institution Press.

Death and Taxes

T axation is made more shameful and burdensome," wrote Salvian the Presbyter in the fifth century AD, "because all do not
bear the burden of all. They extort tribute from the poor man
for the taxes of the rich, and the weaker carry the load for the
stronger." Salvian was complaining of the tax burden imposed on
conquered territory by the Roman Empire, but the same sentiments
might have been expressed by New World peoples as they were incorporated into the expanding Spanish empire.

In a large part of the New World, most notably in regions ruled by
the Aztec and Inca empires, people probably grumbled about taxes
long before the arrival of the Europeans. From the smallest agrarian
chiefdom to empires spanning continents, governments throughout
history have lived off the surplus produced by the populace, and they
have engineered economies to insure that such a surplus was produced. When they conquered the most complex societies of the New
World, the Spaniards substituted their own systems of taxation for
those already in place. How, we may wonder, did the conquistadors
come to the conclusion that New World people owed them anything? Montezuma might have pondered this as he sat under house
arrest in the Spaniards' quarters in Tenochtitlán. For most early Spanish conquerors, however, it was a given.

Columbus took it for granted and had a tribute system in place on
Hispaniola by 1494, as Pietro Martire d'Anghera recorded:

All the natives between the ages of fourteen and seventy years bound
themselves to pay him tribute in the products of the country at so much

per head, promising to fulfill their engagement. Some of the conditions of this agreement were as follows: the mountaineers of Cibao were to bring to the town every three months a specified measure filled with gold. They reckon by the moon and call the months moons. The islanders who cultivated the lands which spontaneously produced spices and cotton, were pledged to pay a fixed sum per head.

Perhaps for sixteenth-century Europeans (as in twentieth-century conventional wisdom), taxes were one of the two inescapable things. Or perhaps Spain, in demanding tribute from conquered peoples, took Rome as its model. Gaul and Britain and Spain itself—or the peoples and lands that then constituted Spain—had paid tribute to Rome a thousand years before Columbus sailed.

Within the Roman system, as in almost all tax systems, the state's objective was to extract a sufficient quantity of money, goods, and services for the least cost. During the period of the Roman republic, the imposition of tribute on conquered territories was an important motivation for the conquests in the first place. Nevertheless, to subjugate the provinces completely and hold them to the letter of tribute demands was probably impossible and certainly not expedient. Conquered territories attempted to minimize their tribute burden without attracting the attention of the imperial army. The Romans, too, were eager to preserve the peace. As Edward Luttwak noted in *The Grand Strategy of the Roman Empire,* "By virtually eliminating the burden of maintaining continuous frontier defenses, the net 'disposable' military power generated by the imperial forces was maximized. Hence, the total military power that others could perceive as being available to Rome for offensive use—and that could therefore be put to political advantage by diplomatic means—was also maximized."

For example, Julius Caesar's strategy for extracting tribute from the province of Gaul depended on convincing local leaders that producing tax revenues was in their interest. In Caesar's words (written in the third person):

> During the winter which he spent in Belgic Gaul Caesar made it his single aim to keep the tribes loyal, and to see that none had any pretext for revolt or any hope of profiting by it. The last thing he wanted was to have to fight a campaign immediately before his departure; for it would mean leaving Gaul in a state of rebellion when the time came to withdraw his army, and all the tribes would be only too willing to take up

Engraving of the native people of Florida bringing presents to a monument erected by the French in the sixteenth century, by Theodor de Bry (from Iacobo le Moyne, Brevis Narratio Eorum Quae in Florida Americae Provincia . . . , 1591. Courtesy of the Benson Latin American Collection)

arms when they could do so without immediate risk. So he made their condition of subjection more tolerable by addressing the tribal governments in complimentary terms, refraining from the imposition of any fresh [tax] burdens, and bestowing rich presents upon the principal citizens. By these means it was easy to induce a people exhausted by so many defeats to live at peace.

Spanish tacticians also knew that much was to be gained by co-opting the local rulers. They coerced and courted them into becoming agents of the empire who would collect tribute and keep the peace. Spain's treatment of its New World territories was similar in other respects to Rome's relationship to its provinces. To generate income, Spain placed the greatest effort in areas of greatest return (such as the gold- and silver-mining regions), just as Rome exploited Britain's mineral wealth. Spain pensioned off its soldiers with grants of New World lands and the labor of conquered people, just as Rome granted parcels of conquered land to retiring soldiers to repay them cheaply and to further subdue the provinces. And like Rome, Spain kept the cost of having an army within bounds by using the threat of force more often than force itself.

As did Rome and Spain, the Inca empire in the Andes undertook its conquests with the smallest standing army possible. In fact one of the most remarkable things about the Inca is how successful they were, given that their army and their original population were so small. But their might was still adequate to subjugate unwilling populations whose traditional leadership had nothing to gain and everything to lose by imperial conquest. And like the Romans, the Inca relied on the cooperation of local elites to fill the imperial coffers.

The Inca policy of gentle persuasion involved taking provincial hostages to the Inca capital, Cuzco, to live in great style. These guests were steeped in the city's language and culture. Undoubtedly, it would have been impressed on them that the treatment they received depended entirely upon their participation in extracting tribute from their homelands. Garcilaso de la Vega, whose mother was a member of the Inca elite and whose father was a Spanish nobleman, described the strategy of the Inca emperor:

> They also carried off the leading chief and all his children to Cuzco, where they were treated with kindness and favor so that by frequenting the court they would learn not only its laws, customs, and correct speech,

but also the rites, ceremonies, and superstitions of the Incas. This done, the [chief] was restored to his former dignity and authority, and the Inca, as king, ordered the vassals to serve and obey him as their natural lord.

The Inca bestowed . . . gifts on newly conquered Indians, so that however brutish and barbarous they had been they were subdued by affection and attached to his service by a bond so strong that no province ever dreamed of rebelling. And in order to remove all occasion for complaint and to prevent dissatisfaction from leading to rebellion, he confirmed and promulgated anew all the former laws, liberties, and statutes so that they might be more esteemed and respected, and he never changed a word of them unless they were contrary to the idolatry and laws of his empire.

The Aztec empire, centered in the capital city Tenochtitlán, also resembled republican Rome in its treatment of peripheral territories. In his book *Trade, Tribute, and Transportation,* the historical anthropologist Ross Hassig emphasized three correspondences in his analysis of the Aztec empire before and during the Spanish conquest:

While the similarities between the Romans and the Aztecs can be overstated, they did share certain characteristics: (1) expansion of political dominance without direct territorial control, (2) a focus on the internal security of the empire by exercising influence on a limited range of activities within the client states, and (3) the achievement of such influence by generally retaining rather than replacing local officials.

When the Inca and Aztec empires fell to Spain, the conquerors seemed in a good position to replace the top strata of New World bureaucratic structures, leaving lower strata intact to funnel tribute upward. But substituting tribute to Spain for tribute to Cuzco or Tenochtitlán was a disaster for several reasons. Foremost, the conquest brought massive loss of life through the introduction of Old World diseases. The indigenous economies were completely disrupted by epidemics that in many areas killed 70 to 90 percent of the population in less than a century, providing a grimly literal example of a shrinking tax base. In the New World, death and taxes were more closely linked than in the proverbial sense.

Second, the expanding European empire did not merely replace the top tier of the indigenous tribute system; it short-circuited the entire structure. Under the Aztec system, for example, tribute flowed through a pyramidal series of institutions, from local governments to regional centers to provincial capitals to Tenochtitlán. With the imposition of Spanish control, these intermediate stops were bypassed; tribute went from local regions directly to Mexico City and from there to Spain. Regional centers and administrative systems withered and disappeared, undercutting the native political order.

Finally, European governments and entrepreneurs were interested in forms of wealth that were tangible and transportable. Taxes in the form of labor—such as the Inca *mita* system, which supplied a workforce for state projects—were less appealing. Thus, local groups that had previously met their obligations by working for the state from time to time were forced to pay tribute in goods.

As bad as this was, the situation was still worse for those New World people who were unaccustomed to life within the sphere of tribute-demanding empires. For them, being forced to pay taxes in the form of money or goods or labor was an impossible order: Little or no surplus was generated by their subsistence economies, and no tribute-collecting mechanisms were in place. As a result, most of these peoples were pushed from their lands or trampled in the course of European expansion.

Today, of course, we enjoy the advantage of governing ourselves, instead of paying tribute to some foreign imperial power. And yet, as Thomas Paine observed in *Common Sense*, "Government even in the best state is but a necessary evil; in its worst state an intolerable one; for when we suffer, or are exposed to the same miseries by a government, which we might expect in a country without government, our calamity is heightened by reflecting that we furnish the means by which we suffer."

Works Cited and Suggestions for Further Reading

Caesar, Julius
1983   *The Conquest of Gaul.* New York: Viking Press.

Hassig, Ross
1975   *Trade, Tribute, and Transportation.* Norman: University of Oklahoma
         Press.

Luttwak, Edward
1976   *The Grand Strategy of the Roman Empire.* Baltimore: Johns Hopkins
         University Press.

Martire de Anghiera, Pietro
1970 [1912]   *De Orbe Novo, the Eight Decades of Peter Martyr d'Anghera.*
                Translated from the Latin with notes and introduction
                by Francis Augustus MacNutt. New York: Burt Franklin.

Paine, Thomas
1987   *Common Sense.* New York: Viking Press (Penguin Classics Reissue
         Edition).

Salvian the Presbyter
1947   *The Writings of Salvian the Presbyter.* New York: Cima.

Vega, Garcilaso de la
1966   *Royal Commentaries of the Incas, and General History of Peru.* Trans-
         lated with an introduction by Harold V. Livermore. Foreword by
         Arnold J. Toynbee. Austin: University of Texas Press.

Pandora's Bite

The Spanish writer Antonio Vásquez de Espinosa, while traveling in the New World tropics in the early 1600s, observed of the environment,

Agreeable as it may be to the sight, seeming a delightful Paradise, to the feeling it is painful in equal degree. Besides the great heat of an excessive intensity, for it is only about 1 degree from the Equator, and the fact that the low-lying country, covered with groves and woods, keeps any wind from circulating, there is an infinity of mosquitoes of numerous varieties, which normally keep travelers in torture; during the day there are gnats and midges which are very painful and stick fast to one's skin, and leave bites that inflame; there are others much tinier which can hardly be made out, but their bites fester; there are others of a sort of blue in color which force travelers by boat during the daytime to stay under canvas, unable to enjoy the lovely scenery of the banks and forests along the great river, whose crystal clear and smoothly running waters make a pleasant and harmonious sound. Then when these pests are sleeping at night, others rise and set sail; these are the night mosquitoes which make an annoying and distressing noise and keep trying to find some part of the canopy through which they can bite the person inside.

While singing around their victims' ears and drawing blood from itching wounds, mosquitoes also spread disease. During the five centuries since Europeans launched the age of exploration, mosquito-borne plagues have laid low both conqueror and conquered, altering the shape of history.

Among the first to offer North American mosquitoes a sample of European blood was Hernando de Soto. Enriched by the part he played in looting the Inca empire of the Andes, he nevertheless was dissatisfied that his name did not command the same respect as that of Pizarro or Cortés, the conquerors of the Inca and the Aztec. De Soto thus set his sights on territory that Europeans had not yet visited, the southeast of what is today the United States. In 1539, he landed an army of more than 600 men near Tampa Bay, Florida, and set off on an armed reconnaissance known as the *entrada*.

The Spaniards first marched by the most direct path from Tampa Bay into the heart of a great swamp, something de Soto seems to have been better at finding during his travels than the gold he so desperately desired. For sixteenth-century Spaniards, as for most Europeans of the era, standing water was equated with dangerous vapors and mosquitoes, both of which were associated with disease. (Like Aristotle in the fourth century BC, Spaniards believed that mosquitoes were spontaneously generated in putrefying waters.) That people lived in such damp and therefore deadly environments in the New World—in Florida, the Caribbean Islands, Central America, and even the Aztec's lake-city of Tenochtitlán—profoundly disturbed the Spaniards.

In three years, de Soto's expedition traveled more than 3,000 miles through territories that now make up eleven states, crossing the Mississippi and going as far west as Texas. It was an imposing company that moved slowly, encamping for many months each winter. When the Spaniards reached the Mississippi, they had to halt for days while they built barges large enough to ferry their horses, armor, weapons, and supplies. Throughout their travels, the Spaniards depended to a great extent on the Indians for food.

In this extraordinary venture, de Soto and his companions saw native North American societies that would never again be witnessed by Europeans. Twenty years later, when Tristan de Luna retraced some of his predecessors' steps, the indigenous people had already been decimated by epidemics of Old World diseases that followed in de Soto's wake. A century later the accounts of de Soto's *entrada* were considered unbelievable: By that time Europeans could not imagine that societies as large and complex as those seen by de Soto had ever existed in North America. This was true in many places in the Americas. The first European explorers unknowingly brought their frightful European diseases with them and large populations were wiped out or drastically reduced in size. Sometimes this effect preceded the Europeans: The story of their arrival would spread before them, and disease would be spread by the ones who brought the news. As a result of disease, the Indian population in many areas had been reduced to a tenth of its preconquest size.

In its turn, de Soto's group succumbed to New World diseases; only about half of those who landed at Tampa Bay lived to tell of their adventures. They died from starvation and Indian arrows and diseases— both those they brought with them and new ones they encountered. There was no gold in the Southeast, but de Soto had become a man possessed, heading north and doubling back to the south, then west and back to the east. As the months stretched into years, his men gave up hope of anything but survival.

Then, in May or June of 1542 (accounts vary as to the exact date), while camped on the banks of the Mississippi, de Soto felt a fever coming on. As it worsened over the next few days, he realized he was dying. No one knows what disease it was, but it was probably a New World malady, since he had survived the ones from the Old World for so long. De Soto wrote his will, "almost in cipher," on a small scrap of paper (since the Spaniards had almost none). He chose his successor, confessed his sins, and died beside the Mississippi, probably in what is now eastern Louisiana.

Without its leader, the expedition tried to head across Texas but turned back when the men found fewer Indians from whom they could commandeer food. Their objective by this time was simply to escape. They built seven small ships and fled down the Mississippi, attacked constantly by well-organized Indian groups.

By then, mosquitoes had fed on de Soto's men so unrelentingly that the insects were rarely mentioned in the *entrada*'s chronicles. But the "Gentleman of Elvas" who traveled with the company recorded the mosquitoes' parting shots:

> The flesh is directly inflamed from their sting, as though it had received venom. Towards morning the wind lulled, and the sea went down; but the insects continued none the less. The sails, which were white, appeared black with them at daylight; while the men could not pull at the oars without assistance to drive away the insects. Fear having passed off with the danger of the storm, the people observing the swollen condition of each other's faces, and the marks of the blows they had given and received to rid them of the mosquitos, they could but laugh. (see also Milanich 1991)

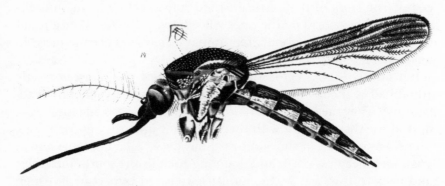

Anopheles mosquito (from P. Wytsman, Genera Insectorum. *Bruxelles: Louis Desmet-Verteneuil, 1931–1933. Courtesy of the Life Sciences Library, University of Texas).*

The Mississippi River was the dividing line for the continent, and the title for its drainage passed several times among European powers. French missionaries and traders explored its length and established trading posts among the Indians of the valley and the Great Plains to the west. In part because of de Soto's expedition, Spain maintained a claim to "Louisiana"—roughly the lands between the Mississippi River and the Rockies. By the end of the eighteenth century, however, Spain's grip had grown weak, and in 1800 Louisiana was ceded to France.

By that time there were new contenders for the territory, for the European colonies on the eastern seaboard of North America had become prosperous and politically independent. They had plans for the lands west of the Mississippi. Seen from a twentieth-century perspective, the Louisiana Purchase is one of Thomas Jefferson's greatest triumphs. Certainly in retrospect it seems like a good buy, as it probably did then—nearly a million square miles, parts of 15 modern states, all for a little more than $11 million. Although this amount of money would have bought much more in 1803 dollars, it still was a bargain at about 2 cents an acre. How clever of Jefferson, and how foolish of Napoleon, to trade what is now some of the world's most valuable real estate for such a sum.

The deal with Jefferson was not, however, exactly what Napoleon had in mind. In 1802, Napoleon sent his brother-in-law Charles

Leclerc with an army of 33,000 men to reinforce France's claim to New Orleans, the port that controlled the territory, and to put down a slave insurrection in Haiti on the way. But 29,000 of the 33,000 men in Leclerc's expedition died of mosquito-borne yellow fever before they could accomplish either objective. Haiti remained free as an African American republic, and the Louisiana Purchase by the United States was arranged in 1803 as a way to salvage something from the failed holding action.

Leclerc's expedition was not the first European colonial power play to be thwarted by disease. In 1585, Sir Francis Drake left Plymouth harbor with 29 ships, 1,500 seamen, and 800 soldiers; his assignment, to disrupt the flow of wealth from the New World to Spain by capturing treasure fleets, destroying ports, and wrecking commercial shipping in the Caribbean. Formerly, Drake had harassed the Spaniards but had never been a real threat. The 1585 expedition was meant to change that, but Drake and his men took on more than food and water when they stopped in the Cape Verde Islands, west of Africa. "Wee were not many dayes at sea," Drake said, "but there beganne amoung our people such mortalitie, as in a fewe days there were dead above two and three hundred men."

Alfred Crosby, in his 1972 book *The Colombian Exchange,* suggested that the disease may have been typhus, but another prime suspect is mosquito-borne yellow fever. Its ten-day gestation period would have allowed Drake to get well out to sea before the epidemic set in. Drake records that "until some seven or eight dayes after our coming from St. Iago, there had not died one man of sicknesse in all the fleete: the sicknesse shewed not her infection wherewith so many were stroked untill we were departed thence, and then seazed our people with extreme hot burning and continual agues." Before they even saw a Spanish ship, Drake's company was already greatly weakened.

Similarly, in 1741 English rulers and strategists attempted to change the political structure of the Americas with one bold stroke. Sensing Spain's weakening hold on her colonies, they sent Admiral Edward Vernon from Southampton with 27,000 men to topple Spain's New World empire. But Vernon engaged mosquitoes and yellow fever instead—possibly in the Canary Islands—and lost 20,000 of his men to the quick killer the Spanish called the black vomit.

How is it that Europeans were ambushed in midocean by Old World diseases? Part of the answer is that Europe's expansion involved not only movement to and from the New World but also contact with Africa, India, Southeast Asia, and China. As travel and trade increased, diseases that had evolved among relatively isolated human groups were carried throughout most of the world, killing Europeans, soldiers on warships crossing the Atlantic, Native Americans, and Africans brought to the New World. The result was what the French historian Emmanuel Le Roi Ladurie has called the "unification of the globe by disease."

Europe's expansion had opened a Pandora's box of diseases. Among these were malaria and yellow fever, neither of which was present in the New World in pre-Columbian times. Even Africans taken by force to the New World, who brought some immunity to tropical fevers with them, suffered great mortality from the unprecedented collection of diseases. In 1647 and 1648, when a plantation system using African slave labor was just being established in the Lesser Antilles, 6,000 people in Barbados—both Africans and Europeans—died of yellow fever. Saint Kitts was also hit, and Guadeloupe had a similar epidemic in 1649.

The exploration of new lands, for all the wealth it was thought to bring, did not enhance the Europeans' life expectancy. Staying far away from the enterprise might have been the most prudent course. Of those on de Soto's expedition, the most fortunate conquistador may have been Vasco Porcallo de Figueroa, who had the wisdom to withdraw early on.

An older man who had already accumulated a modest fortune in the conquest of the New World, Porcallo showed no lack of determination during the early days of the *entrada*. At one point, against the better judgment of de Soto, Porcallo set out to attack and capture the Indian chief Hirrihigua, who had proved uncooperative. When his small company ran into problems crossing a swamp, Porcallo took matters into his own hands:

> As an experienced soldier, he was aware that the most satisfactory means for a captain to command obedience in difficult situations is to lead the way himself, even though he display rashness in doing so. Thus he gave the spurs to his mount, and rushing into the marsh was followed by a number of his companions. He had proceeded only a few steps, however, when his horse fell with him at a spot where both stood a chance of being drowned. . . . Indeed all risked the same danger, but that of Vasco Porcallo was much greater since he was loaded with arms

and enveloped in mud and in addition had caught one leg beneath his horse in such a way that the animal was drowning him without affording him an opportunity to save himself. (Vega 1988)

Porcallo survived, however. Covered in mud and disgusted with himself, his horse, La Florida in its as yet unknown entirety, and the Indian chief who had lured him into such a quagmire, he ordered his men to retreat to their former camp without him. He made the slow, wet walk back alone, weighing his options, feeling his age, and perhaps foreseeing the difficulties that ultimately would defeat de Soto and his army. Porcallo remembered his great property and the ease and comfort he would enjoy at home. All the future labors of the conquest, instead, would be like those he had just experienced or even worse. Perhaps slapping at a bloodthirsty mosquito, he resolved to return to Spain and leave the expedition to younger men.

Works Cited and Suggestions for Further Reading

Cook, Noble David
1998   *Born to Die: Disease and New World Conquest, 1492–1650*. Cambridge, UK: Cambridge University Press.

Crosby, Alfred
1972   *The Colombian Exchange*. Westport, CT: Greenwood.

Drake, Sir Francis
1981   *Sir Francis Drake's West Indian Voyage, 1585–1586*. Edited by Mary Frear Keeler. London: Hakluyt Society.

Elvas, The Gentleman of
1965 [1907]   *Spanish Explorers in the Southern United States, 1528–1543*. New York: Barnes & Noble (reprint edition).

Milanich, Jerald T. (ed.)
1991   *The Hernando de Soto Expedition*. Edited with an introduction by Jerald T. Milanich. New York: Garland.

Vásquez de Espinosa, Antonio
1942   *Compendium and Description of the West Indies*. Translated by Charles Upson Clark. Washington, DC: Smithsonian Institution.

Vega, Garcilaso de la
1988   *The Florida of the Inca*. Austin: University of Texas Press.

The Matter
of Smallpox

In April 1806, a package containing dried scabs and a vial of pus, taken from the open sores of a child in Mexico City, was sent by messenger to Manuel Antonio Cordero y Bustamante, governor of the Spanish provinces surrounding the missions of San Antonio, in what is now Texas. Governor Cordero's physicians lanced the skins of several hundred European Americans and Indians living in the area and smeared the diluted pus and dissolved scabs into the wounds. As a consequence, these residents contracted cowpox, a disease closely related to smallpox. The antibodies they developed from the infection were to protect them from smallpox for the rest of their lives.

Distribution of the vaccine to this outpost of the Spanish empire was due largely to the efforts of Francisco Xavier Balmis, a physician who sailed around the globe between 1803 and 1807 visiting settlements of the Spanish empire. He was among the most courageous of souls not only because of the magnitude of his undertaking—more than 100,000 people in Latin America were vaccinated directly or indirectly through his efforts—but also because he struggled, along with many others, against the popularly held, intuitive sentiment that one did not preserve people's health by making them sick.

In a 1941–1942 article in *The Bulletin of the History of Medicine*, S. F. Cook related how the Spanish king Carlos IV, terrified when his daughter contracted smallpox, had the rest of his family vaccinated after she recovered. Then, at his government's expense, he mounted

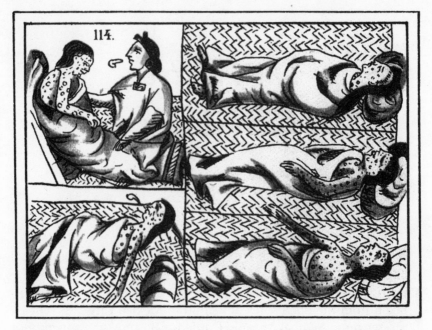

Smallpox (from the Lienzo de Tlaxcala. *Courtesy of the Benson Latin American Collection, University of Texas).*

the "philanthropic expedition of vaccination," putting Balmis in charge of getting the vaccine across the Atlantic to North and South America, and if possible, on to the Spanish Philippines. At the time, it was by far the largest vaccination program ever attempted. On the first leg of his journey, Balmis sailed from Spain to the Canary Islands and then to Puerto Rico.

Carrying the vaccine across the Atlantic was not easy. To vaccinate others, Balmis needed the "matter" of cowpox from the open sores of infected people—what we now know to be the active virus. That meant that he needed the pus and lymphatic fluid from people who were at just the right stage of the disease. Once infected, a victim showed no symptoms for more than a week. Aches, fever, and delirium set in about the ninth day, and at the beginning of the third week after exposure, blisters and pustules erupted.

So from the orphanages of Coruna, Spain, and surrounding areas, Balmis recruited twenty-two young boys who had never had either cowpox or smallpox. He then saw to it that they were infected with cowpox one by one as they crossed the ocean and traveled through Latin America, ensuring that there would always be one person whose infection was at the right stage to pass on the disease. These twenty-two children were rewarded with the Crown's commitment to care for them until they were grown and to pay the costs of their schooling in the New World. Although little is known about how these children fared in the Americas or whether any of them ever returned to Spain, none of them died from their exposure to the disease, and they saved thousands.

Balmis's expedition was inspired by the work of the English physician Edward Jenner, who demonstrated that a patient could gain immunity against smallpox relatively safely by being infected with cowpox, a less dangerous disease that rarely proved fatal. In 1796, Jenner inoculated a child with pus taken from a cowpox sore on the hand of a milkmaid, who had caught it from an open sore on the udder of a cow. As Jenner records in a letter to a friend, "But now listen to the most delightful part of my story. The boy has since been inoculated for the Smallpox which as I ventured to predict produced no effect. I shall now pursue my Experiments with redoubled ardor."

Jenner was not the first to notice that contracting cowpox could save a person from getting a fatal version of smallpox later. It was part of local knowledge in rural Britain. Milkmaids routinely caught cowpox; afterward, they almost never contracted smallpox. But Jenner's experiments convinced the medical community that immunization was the best way of fighting smallpox and made cowpox the method of choice.

For centuries people had known that if you survived a bout with smallpox itself, you could almost never catch it again. They believed, often mistakenly, that a person who contracted smallpox through the skin, in the same way that milkmaids caught cowpox through the cuts or calluses on their hands, had a good chance of survival. They also thought that those who caught the disease from close contact with an infected person (evidently by inhaling the virus) were more likely to die or to have their bodies pitted and scarred by the pox.

Inoculation with smallpox itself, also called variolation, appears to have been common for centuries among rural populations throughout Europe, Asia, and Africa. Correspondence in the archives of the

Doorway to the chapel of the Mission San José, San Antonio, Texas.

Royal Society of London shows that English travelers had observed the practice in China before 1700. Several generations before Jenner's experiments, a furious debate had raged among physicians and town councils in Europe and America over whether inoculation with the "matter" of smallpox should be allowed. In the 1720s, in Boston and other New England towns, a war of pamphlets and posters was waged for and against the practice.

Inoculation was a chancy procedure. About 1.5 percent of those inoculated contracted severe cases and died of the disease, and sometimes recently inoculated people, who had not been kept in quarantine while they were contagious, spread the disease to others. But smallpox was such a ghastly disease that to avoid it people were willing to risk death for themselves and their children. In 1634, William Bradford provided an appalling description of what smallpox did to the Connecticut Indians:

> They fell sick of ye small poxe, and dyed most miserably; for a sorer disease cannot befall them; they fear it more than ye plague; for usualy they that have this disease have them in abundance, and for wante of bedding and lining and other helps, they fall into a lamentable condition, as they lye on their hard matte ye poxe breaking and mattering, and runing one into another, their skin cleaving (by reason thereof) to the matts they lye on; when they trn them, a whole side will flea of at once, (as it were) and they will be all of a gore blood, most fearful to behold; and then being very sore, what with could and other distempers, they dye like rotten sheep.

Later, Bradford notes that seeing the Indians' "woefull and sadd condition, and hearing their pitifull cries and lamantations, [the settlers] had compastion of them, and dayly fetched them wood and water, and made them fires, gott them victualls whilst they lived, and buried them when they dyed."

The Puritan minister and prolific writer Cotton Mather (1663–1728) learned of smallpox inoculation from a man named Onisemus, who had been brought as a slave from Africa. Mather asked other people from Africa about the practice and found that it was commonly done there. Given the tremendous threat of smallpox epidemics in the new American colonies, he became a strong proponent of inoculation with smallpox. In his small book titled *An Account of the Method and Success of Inoculating the Small-Pox,* printed in London in 1722, he gave a step-by-step description of the procedure:

> They make a Choice of as healthy a young Person as they can find, that has the SmallPox of the best Sort upon him; on the Twelfth or Thirteenth Day of his Decumbiture, with a Needle they prick some of the larger Pustules, and press out the Matter coming from them into some convenient Vessel, which is to be stopt close, and kept warm, in the Bosom of the Person that carries it to the intended Patient. This Person ought rather to be some other, than he who visited the sick Chamber for it; lest he should carry the Infection in the common way, which might prove dangerous. The Patient is to have several Small Wounds made with a Needle, or Lancet, in two or more places of the Skin, (the best Places are the Muscles of the Arm) and immediately let there be dropt out of a Drop of the Matter in the Glass on each of the Places, and mix'd with the Blood that is issuing out. The Wound should be cover'd with some little Concave Vessel, and bound over, that the Matter may not be rubb'd off by the garments for a few Hours.

The dedication to Mather's book, written by J. Dummer, affirmed that the idea that inoculation with smallpox could prevent the disease was not at all new:

> This Practice of ingrafting the Small-Pox has been used from Time immemorial among the Circassians, and for many Years past in the Levant, yet it is a new Thing in these Parts of Europe, and still more so in America: And as all new Discoveries, however rational in themselves, and beneficial to Mankind, are receiv'd at first with Opposition, none has met with greater than this in New-England.

In the late 1600s, the practice of inoculation with smallpox had been described in Turkey and the eastern Mediterranean, and seems to have been widely used throughout Europe. Peasants called the rather dangerous practice "buying the smallpox," and most contemporary accounts noted (with either praise or contempt) that old women were the ones who knew how to inoculate people. A highly respected London physician of the early eighteenth century, for example, wrote derisively that "posterity will scarcely be brought to believe that a method practiced only by a few Ignorant Women, amongst an illiterate and unthinking People should ... be received into the Royal Palace" (quoted in Sterns 1950).

Even though these practices existed, no one at the time understood why the disease spread or why inoculation seemed to work sometimes. Classical Greek physicians like Hippocrates based their treatments on the premise that diseases arose from imbalances in the four basic humors, a theory still current in the seventeenth century. The humors were blood, yellow bile, black bile, and mucus (the sanguine, choleric, melancholic, and phlegmatic humors, respectively). Disequilibrium among these humors was thought to cause the skin to erupt with the sores of smallpox, but just what caused the disequilibrium was unclear.

The celebrated Muslim physician Abu Bakr Muhammad ibn Zakariya Razi (better known as Rhazes), who lived from about AD 865 to 925, built upon the humoral theory of disease by suggesting that within each of us there is a case of smallpox (and many other maladies) waiting to boil out of our blood and erupt into open sores on the skin. His "innate seed theory" also involved the belief that changes in atmospheric conditions could trigger epidemics. Even into the nineteenth century this theory was probably the most widely accepted explanation for why people got sick (little wonder that Spanish conquistadors were so obsessed with the risks of staying in the "unhealthful airs" of the American tropics).

Although these humoral and innate seed explanations were widely accepted, a remarkably modern theory was proposed as early as 1546 by an Italian from Verona, Girolamo Fracastoro (1478–1553). In his *De Contagione et Contagiosis Morbis et Eorum Curatione,* he argued that seminaria—in effect small seeds of disease—could be transmitted from person to person through a variety of means. Each disease (he addressed measles and smallpox specifically) had its own unique seminaria. Fracastoro also spent much of his career studying "the French disease"—syphilis.

After the Dutch businessman and amateur lens grinder Anton van Leeuwenhoek (1632–1723) refined the single-lens microscope in the seventeenth century, the existence of microscopic organisms was demonstrated, and Fracastoro's theory of seminaria was revived in a new form. About the same time, a theory attributing the spread of smallpox to animalcules (minuscule animals) was also widely discussed. The smallpox virus was so minute, however, that it was not detected with the early microscopes. Thus for a time such explanations remained in doubt. In some of his writings, for example, Cotton Mather called the agents of the disease "animalculae" of uncertain character, but in others he called them "miasms" (miasmas, or vapors).

"The venomous Miasms of the Small Pox," Mather wrote, "entering into the Body, in the Way of Inspiration, are immediately taken into the Blood of the Lungs; and, I pray, how many Pulses pass, before the very Heart is pierc'd with them? And within how many more they are convey'd into all the Bowels?" In an elaborate discussion he compared the body to a fortress and argued that if the miasms came in through the lungs, they were deadly, but if they had to fight their way through the "Out-Works of the Citadel," the person's skin and muscle, they could be defeated.

But where did the miasmas come from? In the early 1700s, no one knew. The English physician Thomas Sydenham (1642–1689)—whose opinions, so powerful in the inoculation debates in Boston in the 1720s, were well known to Mather—believed that "noxious miasms" issuing forth from the earth into the atmosphere were responsible for epidemics. Sydenham's 1666 treatise *Methodus Curandi Febres* was based on this "miasmic theory" and was the most influential reference available in its day.

The treatments that doctors used to treat smallpox, however, had little to do with the theories of how the patient got the disease. Rhazes believed that imperceptible atmospheric changes brought illness and advocated "heat therapy" to warn the body of an invisible threat and drive away the infectious humors. Fracastoro believed that seminaria had somehow entered the patient's body and went along with Rhazes in hoping that heat might drive them out again. Sydenham's theory did not contribute to the understanding of how people got smallpox, but rather to its clinical treatment. He argued that heat therapy with steam and blankets was the worst treatment as it exacerbated the sores and helped to spread the contagion.

From the idea that diseases were spread through microscopic seeds or animalcules, it was a small step to understanding that different diseases were brought about by very different animalcules. "The Pestilence can never breed the Small-Pox, nor the Small-Pox the Measles any more than a Hen can a Duck, a Wolf a Sheep, or a thistle Figs," wrote the physician Thomas Fuller in his 1772 *Pharmacopoeia Extemporainea*. Bacteriology and modern "germ theories" of disease were based on these concepts and were further refined in the 1870s by pioneers like Robert Koch and Louis Pasteur.

Only in the twentieth century have scientists begun to learn how viruses invade the human organism and how the immune system can learn to identify and repel new threats. We now believe that vaccination with cowpox confers immunity to smallpox because the two are related members of a family of viruses, which also includes monkeypox, camelpox, buffalopox, and whitepox.

Although Jenner's method of vaccination became widespread, smallpox was extremely difficult to eradicate. Immunity cannot be passed on from one generation to another, so each new generation is vulnerable to smallpox epidemics. In a letter to Jenner, Thomas Jefferson wrote, "Yours is the comfortable reflection that mankind can never forget that you have lived. Future nations will know by history only that the loathsome smallpox has existed." He was right about the first part, but it took nearly two centuries to make the second part a reality (see Fenner et al. 1988).

Just as Francisco Xavier Balmis needed a human chain of orphaned children to maintain an active cowpox infection during his Atlantic crossing, smallpox must spread from person to person in order to continue to exist naturally. By 1977, after a decade of intensive vaccination led by the World Health Organization, the virus was unable to find its next victim. Although a cure for smallpox had never been found, the disease was conquered.

Yet the virus is still maintained in laboratories for study. (In 1978, it escaped from a British laboratory, several people were infected, and one of them died.) Samples of the virus still sit in freezers in Moscow and at the Centers for Disease Control in Atlanta. Should we now keep it alive? The DNA sequences of several strains of the virus are known, and if need be, the virus could be reconstructed using nucleotide sequences from other organisms. Thus, some argue that we should destroy the remaining samples. But if we keep them frozen, we may be able to learn more from them later. As one of the oldest and wisest of human adages says, keep your friends close and your enemies closer. The World Health Organization has decided not to dispose of the last samples just yet.

Works Cited and Suggestions for Further Reading

Bradford, William
1966 [1952]   *Of Plimoth Plantation, 1620–1647*. New York: Alfred A.
                 Knopf.

Cook, S. F.
1941–1942   Francisco Xavier Balmis and the Introduction of
                 Vaccine. . . .*Bulletin of the History of Medicine,* v11,
                 p543–557; v12, p70–89.

Fenner, Frank, et al. (eds.)
1988   *Smallpox and Its Eradication*. Geneva: World Health Organization.

Hopkins, Donald R.
1983   *Princes and Peasants: Smallpox in History.* Chicago: University of
         Chicago Press.

Miller, Genevieve (ed.)
1983   *The Letters of Edward Jenner.* Baltimore: Johns Hopkins University
         Press.

Public Health in America
1977   *Smallpox in Colonial America.* New York: Arno Press.

Sterns, R. P.
1950   Remarks upon the Introduction of Inoculation for Smallpox in En-
         gland. *Bulletin of the History of Medicine.*

"That Unmanned, Wild Countrey"

In the mid-1600s, the English settlers who had gained a foothold along the eastern seaboard of North America began to make a profit by growing Native American tobacco and selling it in European markets. This kind of enterprise demanded farmland, and even more land was needed by the increasing tide of colonists arriving in the mid-Atlantic states and New England. But the land from Florida to Maine was occupied by American Indians—numbering in the hundreds of thousands—who lived in permanent villages, hunted wild game in well-defined hunting territories, and grew crops in fields that were shifted in a regular pattern as the fertility of the soil declined.

The English colonists came up with two justifications for taking the Native Americans' lands. First, they argued that colonists would civilize the Indians and "cover their naked miserie, with civill use of foode and cloathing." In royal charters given to the companies organizing the colonization, mention was always made of the obligation to bring Christianity to the "savages." The other part of the rationale was that Europeans could put the land to a "higher use," making it more productive by intensive cultivation and by bringing in livestock. In 1625, Samuel Purchas, a compiler of many important documents, argued that God did not intend for the land to remain as "that unmanned wild Countrey, which [the savages] range rather than inhabited."

In early laws in Virginia and Massachusetts, and in many recorded sermons, biblical passages were quoted as justification for the appropriation of land: "Ask of me, and I shall give thee the heathen for thine inheritance, and the uttermost parts of the earth for thy possession" (Psalms 2:8); and, "Whosoever, therefore, resisteth the power, resisteth the ordinance of God; and they that resist shall receive to themselves damnation" (Romans 13:2). A contemporary satirist (who wisely chose to remain anonymous) put it succinctly in a supposed summary of a Puritan town meeting: "Voted, that the earth is the Lord's and the fulness thereof; Voted, that the earth is given to the Saints; Voted, that we are the Saints."

The idea that land could be taken if it was not being used as the English would use it, or if the people on it were "uncivilized" or not of the proper religion, was not new. In the late 1500s, the English had conquered parts of Ireland on the same pretext. In 1973, the Irish historian Nicholas Canny noted that even though England and Ireland were similar in religion and land use, the Irish quickly came to be viewed as uncivilized people, even as cannibals (a charge that proved effective in mobilizing force against Indians as well): "Once it was established that the Irish were pagans, the first logical step had been taken toward declaring them barbarians."

The idea that Europeans might put the land to higher use required downplaying how the native people were using it. This was somewhat problematic because the land the settlers desired most was the best land, that which the Indians had already cleared for their own crops of beans, corn, pumpkins, squash, and tobacco. The English were able, however, to construct an image of the Indians as nomadic hunters who did not change the landscape. According to the historian Francis Jennings, when the lawyer John Winthrop took control of an English company in the Atlantic colonies in 1630, he declared that "most land in America was vacuum domicilium—i.e., legally 'waste'—because the Indians had not 'subdued' it by methods recognized in English law and therefore had no 'natural' right to it; the alternative of 'civil' right was impossible for Indians because they did not have civil government. In operational terms civil government meant European government" (Jennings 1975).

Later, in the eighteenth century, Enlightenment thinkers such as Rousseau saw the Indians as "noble savages" who lived at one with nature, without want, greed, or possessiveness, untainted by contact with civilization. The eloquent and influential nineteenth-century historian Francis Parkman believed that the Indian was "a true child of the forest and the desert. The wastes and solitudes of nature are his congenial home." In this way, the Indians were nearly defined out of existence, allowing the frontier historian Frederick Jackson Turner, in 1920, to say that the West had been "free land" and Walter Prescott Webb, in 1931, to refer to it as "land free to be taken."

But New World people had changed the landscape, often in ways the European colonists did not appreciate. Along the east coast of North America, the lands that the English sought for tobacco cultivation had been planted for thousands of years. As fertility declined in some fields, the Indians opened up others, leaving the older ones to lie fallow. Later they might return to previously used fields, whose overgrowth of brush and small trees was easier to clear than climax forest. By the time the colonists arrived, the eastern woodlands had become a mosaic of Indian fields, some in use, some overgrown with brush, some nearly forests again.

Fire was a useful tool for renovating farming plots: It not only cleared the undergrowth but it also returned nutrients from the vegetation to the soil. Indians used fire widely in eastern North America to change the nature of the forests. English settlers recorded a marked shift in the forest vegetation after the Indians retreated farther west. At first the forest was described as "parklands," with little vegetation at ground level. After the Indians died or moved away, the Europeans began to describe the forest as dense and scrubby, with impenetrable thickets of vegetation beneath the woodland canopy.

Native Americans had used controlled burning to limit the growth of the understory, thus making it easier to hunt, collect wild foods such as hickory nuts and acorns, and cultivate the land. They knew that deer and the other animals they hunted thrived on plants that grew after the forest floor was burned. Prehistoric land-use patterns can be reconstructed through archeological excavation and the analysis of preserved plant pollen. The archeologist Jefferson Chapman and paleoecologists Hazel Delcourt and Paul Delcourt, for example, have charted 10,000 years of human impact on the environments of eastern Tennessee (Delcourt and Delcourt 1989).

Farther west, Native Americans used fires to turn forests into grasslands and, in drier areas, to keep prairies from becoming chaparral or scrub deserts. In a 1980 article, "Indian Fires of Spring," the archeolo-

The seal of the Massachusetts Bay Company.
The voice ribbon above the Indian's head reads,
"Come over and help us."

gist Henry Lewis described how, for millennia, the Indians modified landscapes in Alberta, and how present-day environmental agencies are rediscovering the advantages of controlled burning. The catastrophic fires in Yellowstone National Park in the summer of 1988 showed that fire is an inherent part of the forest ecosystem, without which some species cannot survive or reproduce. They also showed the dangers of suppressing natural fires for decades.

In what is now the southwestern United States and northern Mexico, people rerouted the flow of rivers to create environments capable of supporting large populations. For example, in about AD 1000, Hohokam Indians built an elaborate system of canals and irrigated fields in the floodplains of the Gila and Salt Rivers (south of modern Phoenix). On a larger scale, Middle and South American peoples, such as the Aztecs, the Incas, and their predecessors, transformed landscapes with thousands of miles of canals and extensive drained or irrigated fields.

The possibility that early Native Americans were responsible for the extinction of the large animals of the Western Hemisphere has been hotly debated by archeologists and vertebrate paleontologists for the past thirty years. Many of the animals that were around at the end of the last glaciation 12,000 years ago—mastodons, giant sloths, camels, giant beavers, and many more—disappeared soon after the climate warmed. The weapons and butchering tools found with the bones of these animals make it hard to argue that humans played no role in these extinctions. In the Caribbean the extermination of such species as giant flightless owls can be more closely tied to the arrival of the first humans. Like the giant flightless birds of New Zealand, the owls had no defenses against human predation.

Whereas some scholars have documented the effect New World peoples had on their environment, others have sought to cast them as primitive conservationists, people who knew the inner workings of ecosystems and lived without changing them. This view, which emerged in the nineteenth century, gained widespread favor in this century. For example, in "Aboriginal Conservators," a 1938 article in *Bird Lore,* the anthropologist Frank Speck wrote,

> Do uncivilized tribes know the virtues of conservation? The question would seem to require an answer in the negative in view of what is generally believed to represent the intelligence standard of peoples who have not reached the status of advanced civilization. Surprising though it may seem, the answer is, nevertheless, in the affirmative so far as the eastern and northern forests of the continent are concerned.

More recently, former Secretary of the Interior Stewart L. Udall declared that "the Indians were, in truth, the pioneer ecologists of this country." And a television spot makes use of this imagery: It shows an unidentified American Indian wearing a strange mixture of plains and woodland clothes, paddling a canoe (from yet another area), and beholding modern pollution with tears in his eyes.

People who call Native Americans conservationists probably intend this as a compliment to their sophistication. The ability to wreak havoc on the environment is no longer regarded as a measure of civilization. But this compliment retains a note of condescension, assuming that Europeans had the ability to subdue the land, even if unwisely, whereas native peoples merely adapted to it, finding ways of surviving without changing things. In other words, for the Indians, environments shaped cultures, but for Europeans, cultures shaped environments.

The disdainful argument that Native Americans did not destroy the land simply because they did not have the means to do so was put forward in 1969 by the historian Peter Farb, who wrote,

> If the Northern Athabaskan and Northern Algonkian Indians husbanded the land and its wildlife in primeval times, it was only because they lacked both the technology to kill very many animals and the market for so many furs. But once White traders entered the picture, supply-

ing the Indians with efficient guns and an apparently limitless market for furs beyond the Seas, the Indians went on an orgy of destruction.

This orgy of destruction, however, was introduced by European Americans; the Indian participation is strong evidence that the traditional cultural values of northern forest peoples had eroded by the eighteenth century. The historian Calvin Martin, in *Keepers of the Game* (1978), discusses some of the cultural mechanisms that prevented overexploitation even during the fur trade. "The single most important deterrent to excessive hunting," he argues, "was the fear of spiritual reprisal for indiscreet slaughter. Prior to European influence, these Indians of the Canadian forest were on amicable terms with the spirits of the game, including the game 'bosses,' or keepers of the game, and it was the vivid, daily awareness of this courteous relationship which more than anything else precluded overkill."

This view may be greatly oversimplified, as demonstrated in a collection of papers titled *Indians, Animals, and the Fur Trade: A Critique of Keepers of the Game* (Krech 1981). The idea that people refrained from doing things that they were in every way capable of doing only because of what some may characterize as "superstition" ignores another more plausible option—that they could, but chose not to.

Still, in preconquest North America, people believed that spirits or living essences inhabited what most Western folk hold to be inanimate objects. As the Ojibwa writer William Jones observed of his own people in 1861, "They suppose that all animals, fish, trees, stones, etc., are endued with immortal spirits and that they possess supernatural power to punish any one who may dare despise or make any unnecessary waste of them."

Native Americans have been conceived of in many ways, as both savage and noble. The latest stereotype, as "ecological Indians," oversimplifies their interaction with their environment. The important lesson they offer is that they changed the New World continents in ways that made the land more productive, and yet they carefully avoided the destruction of the ecosystems of the Americas.

Works Cited and Suggestions for Further Reading

Butzer, Karl W. (guest editor)
1992   The Americas Before and After 1492: Current Geographical Research. *Annals of the Association of American Geographers*, v83, n3. Washington, DC: Association of American Geographers.

Canny, Nicholas
1973   The Ideology of English Colonization: From Ireland to America. *William & Mary Quarterly,* 3rd Ser., v30, p575–598.

Delcourt, Hazel, and Paul Delcourt
1989   Strawberry Fields, Almost Forever. *Natural History*, September 1989, p50–60.

Deloria, Vine
1970   *We Talk, You Listen.* New York: Macmillan.

Farb, Peter
1969   *Man's Rise to Civilization: As Shown by the Indians of North America from Primeval Times to the Coming of the Industrial State.* New York: Avon.

Jennings, Francis
1975   *The Invasion of America: Indians, Colonialism, and the Cant of Conquest.* Chapel Hill: Published for the Institute of Early American History and Culture by the University of North Carolina Press.

Jones, William
1982   Ojibwa Texts. In Thomas W. Overholt and J. Baird Callicott (eds.), *Clothed-in-Fur, and Other Tales: An Introduction to an Ojibwa World View*. With Ojibwa texts by William Jones and foreword by Mary B. Black-Rogers. Washington, DC: University Press of America.

Krech III, Shepard (ed.)
1981   *Indians, Animals, and the Fur Trade: A Critique of Keepers of the Game.* Athens: University of Georgia Press.

Lewis, Henry
1980   Indian Fires of Spring. *Natural History*, January 1980, p76–83.

Martin, Calvin
1978   *Keepers of the Game: Indian-Animal Relationships and the Fur Trade.* Berkeley: University of California Press.

Speck, Frank
1938   Aboriginal Conservators. *Bird Lore*, v40, n4, p257–261.

Garcilaso de la Vega, El Inca

T he almost mythical stories of the conquest of the New World, within which seemingly predestined characters like Columbus, Cortés, de Soto, and Pizarro acted out their fates, mask the real character of the times. No one then understood the scope and significance of their enterprise any more than their horses did, and only the vagaries of chance and historical process separated well-known figures like Pizarro and Montezuma from the vast ranks of the European and Native American unknowns.

Among the participants in this complex period were the sons and daughters of Spanish men and Indian women. One was Garcilaso de la Vega, El Inca, who was the child of a Spanish nobleman and an Inca woman in the close family of the Inca kings. The story of Garcilaso's life was determined to a large extent by the social status and political positions of his parents. But his genius transcended the social stigma attached in the sixteenth century and later to those of mixed European and Indian ancestry; Garcilaso de la Vega was to become one of the most sensitive chroniclers of the early contact period and one of the most perceptive and sophisticated scholars of his day.

In July 1528, Sebastián Garcilaso de la Vega, a Spaniard of noble birth, left Spain for the New World as a captain in the company of the conquistador Pedro de Alvarado. In his early years Sebastián appears here and there in the voluminous official records of the Spanish empire. But had the child he had with the Inca noblewoman

Chimpu Ocllo not been so extraordinary, Sebastián's name would barely be noticed among the first Europeans in the New World.

By the early 1530s, Francisco Pizarro, Diego de Almagro, Hernando de Soto, and others in their company had amassed an almost incalculable fortune in looting Peru. Following the method Cortés had used in subduing the Aztec empire in Mexico, they did it by heading almost without resistance for the Inca capital of Cuzco. There they captured, ransomed, baptized, and executed the Inca ruler Atahualpa. The wealth collected in his ransom was enormous, because gold was an important commodity among the Inca elite. As the royal accountant Agustín de Zárate observed,

> They held gold in great esteem, for the king and his chief followers used vessels and wore adornments made of it, and offered it in their temples. The king had a block on which he sat of 16-carat gold: it was worth over twenty-five thousand ducats, and was the article that Don Francisco Pizarro chose as a present for himself at the time of the conquest, for according to his contract he was to receive a present of his own choosing, in addition to his share of the booty as a whole.

Although they found gold and silver in quantities never before seen in the conquest of the New World, the Spaniards believed that the Inca had hidden the vast majority of gold. News of such potential fortune could not be contained, and European fortune seekers throughout the Western Hemisphere were drawn to the Andes. However, even though their portions of Atahualpa's ransom made Pizarro and his colleagues among the richest men in the world, they were determined to keep other Spaniards out of the Inca kingdom. Sebastián Garcilaso de la Vega and his leader Pedro de Alvarado were among the many equally determined to get in.

Alvarado's army of 500 Spaniards, several hundred horses, and several hundred Central American Indians set sail from Nicaragua, landing near the place at which the Isthmus of Panama meets the South American mainland. They undertook a deadly march of nearly 800 miles up into the Andean mountains. Diego de Almagro, sometimes Pizarro's partner and often his competitor, met the army near Quito, Ecuador, and negotiated a private and unrecorded deal with Alvarado that left Pizarro in control of the men and the ships. Alvarado himself left the scene, probably taking for his part a sizable fortune with

Illustration of a Spaniard and an Incan ruler, by Guaman Poma de Ayala, from Historia Gráfica del Perú, *1613.*

him. Sebastián Garcilaso de la Vega went on to Cuzco, the capital of the failing Inca empire, and the seat of Pizarro's growing domain.

The political situation in Peru in the 1530s was highly charged and extremely dangerous. Factional warfare among the Spaniards was nearly constant, and battles were fought both in the Inca centers in the Andes and in the courts of Spain. Almagro and Pizarro's family were at war off and on, and for the Spanish conquerors it was nearly impossible to survive without the support of one or the other of them. Sebastián Garcilaso de la Vega navigated these treacherous times with the mastery of one whose whole life had been spent weighing the political prospects of various leaders and shifting his allegiances in the nick of time. Casting his lot with Pizarro at a time when Almagro still controlled Cuzco, he found himself under a relatively pleasant house arrest for ten months in 1537. The Pizarro family soon regained the upper hand, and for his loyalty Sebastián was awarded a sizable grant, consisting of the land and labor of the people of the Inca province of Cochapampa.

Children who traced their ancestry to both the New World and Europe were a positive product of the conquest. Some came from informal or unconscionable unions, but many were the offspring of formal and long-lived marriages. Unlike people from some other European nations, Spaniards of high birth or high aspirations valued a person's status and social class far more than any abstract classifications of "race." The Marquis Don Francisco Pizarro, the conqueror of Peru, had a child with Doña Angelina, daughter of the Incan king Atahualpa. Their son was named Francisco. Pizarro was evidently as uncreative when it came to naming children as he was enticed by the Inca nobility, for by another Inca noblewoman, Doña Inés Huaillas Ñuestra, he had a daughter whom he named Doña Francisca. This daughter later married Hernando Pizarro, her uncle. Doña Inés eventually left Pizarro and married another Spaniard, Martín de Ampuero. (For the involved details of these and other marriages, see Garcilaso de la Vega's *Royal Commentaries of the Incas, and General History of Peru*.)

Garcilaso de la Vega was also the child of both Spanish and Inca nobility. His father was Sebastián Garcilaso de la Vega and his mother was Ñusta Chimpu Ocllo, the niece of the king Huiyna Cápac, from whom before the conquest Atahualpa had stolen the Inca throne. Without delving too far into the Machiavellian politics of the preconquest Inca aristocracy, it can be noted that Chimpu Ocllo was a lucky survivor of the illegitimate Atahualpa's purge of his royal competitors. This internal dissension among the Inca elite played into the hands of Pizarro, who was viewed by some as a figure sent to extract revenge for Atahualpa's massacre of the legitimate heirs to the Inca throne.

Young Garcilaso's education was more like that of a Spanish nobleman's son than that of an Inca prince. He learned to ride and joust; to hunt with falcons; and to read and write in Spanish, Latin, and Italian. But Garcilaso also spoke his mother's tongue, Quechua, and lived in his mother's house. This house was, by Garcilaso's detailed descriptions, a haven for the dispossessed Inca elite, and much of his massive work *The Royal Commentaries of the Incas* was written from recollections of what he heard in his mother's house. Born in April 1539, Garcilaso witnessed the last gasps of the old Inca order and knew well members of the last Inca generation that had lived before the arrival of Europeans.

In his writings it is clear that Garcilaso rejected neither part of his ancestry. His message—the point that pervades his narrations of the deeds of Inca kings in the *Royal Commentaries* and of Hernando de Soto's expedition in the North American southeast in *The Florida of the Inca*—was that Indians were human beings equal to Europeans in the eyes of God. In his preface to the *Florida,* he says that he is "under obligation to two races, since I am the son of a Spanish father and an Indian mother." He takes pride in calling himself mestizo, and implicit in his writings is a subtle chauvinism that a son of both races might in fact be just a little bit superior to the product of either one alone. But although Garcilaso was not racist in the least, he was the product of two cultural traditions within which social rank and position were all important. He believed unabashedly in superior and inferior classes, and being born to nobility on both sides, clearly saw himself in the former category. For him the tragedy of his later life was that other Spanish nobles did not see it that way.

In his writings Garcilaso de la Vega is unswervingly pro-Christian and usually pro-Spanish. Although for Garcilaso the Indians were equal in aptitude and capabilities, they were disadvantaged by lack of schooling and by not being Christians. Therefore (at least in his writings for the Spanish upper class) he did not condemn the conquest of the New World and portrayed the tragedies that went along with it as positive for the Indians in the long run. Here Garcilaso, who has been almost a messianic figure for generations of New World people, shows himself in the most questionable light. His writings, produced for an exclusive audience and under exceptional circumstances, show most clearly the difficult decisions and mixed allegiances that go along with being caught between two worlds, accepted by neither. He threw his energies into dealing with his father's people and faced the difficulty of arguing the case of Indian equality for a curious but strongly biased audience. He ends his preface to *The Florida of the Inca* saying,

I plead now that this account be received in the same spirit as I present it, and that I be pardoned its errors because I am an Indian. For since we Indians are a people who are ignorant and uninstructed in the arts and sciences, it seems ungenerous to judge our deeds and utterances strictly in accordance with the precepts of those subjects which we have not

learned. We should be accepted as we are. And although I may not deserve such esteem, it would be a noble and magnanimous idea to carry
this merciful consideration still further and to honor in me all of the
mestizo Indians and the creoles of Peru, so that seeing a novice of their
own race receive the favor and grace of the wise and learned, they
would be encouraged to make advancements with similar ideas drawn
from their own uncultivated mental resources. I trust therefore that the
noble in understanding and the liberal in spirit will offer their favor
most generously and approvingly to both my people and myself, for my
desire and willingness to serve them (as my poor works, both past and
present reveal, and as my future works will show) well deserve their consideration.

Nevertheless, Garcilaso is one of the most important chroniclers of
the encounter of two worlds. The *Royal Commentaries* offer access to
the Inca elites' perceptions of the conquest, and *The Florida of the
Inca,* even though Garcilaso was not involved in de Soto's expedition,
is marked by a sympathy with the situation confronted by the southeastern Indians that other accounts lack. In his foreword to the 1966
edition of *The Royal Commentaries of the Incas,* the world historian
Arnold Toynbee likens Garcilaso to other great cultural interpreters:

> He interpreted to the Western aggressors the history and institutions
> and ideas and ideals of one of the civilizations that those aggressors
> were victimizing. In this role, Garcilaso had some famous predecessors.
> The West's impact on the world in and after the sixteenth century of the
> Christian Era had a precedent in the Greeks' impact on the world in and
> after the fourth century B.C. This Greek impact on contemporary Orien-
> tal civilizations evoked in each of these an intelligentsia that interpreted
> its ancestral civilization to the Greeks in Greek terms. The Babylonian
> civilization was interpreted to the Greeks by Berossus; the Egyptian, by
> Manetho; the Jewish, by Philo and by Josephus. This is a distinguished
> company to which Garcilaso belongs.

Garcilaso left Peru at the age of 21 and never returned. When his father died he received a bequest with which he was to go to Spain, greet
his relatives, and continue his education. The reception he received
was cool. The blood of Inca kings in his veins meant only illegitimacy
to his Spanish relations. There was little land or fortune to claim in
Spain, as his father Sebastián had been the third son in a family of nine
children. Like many children of conquistadors he made a petition to

the Royal Council of the Indies, arguing in effect that his father's efforts had made Spain the richest nation in Europe, but that his noble children were undercompensated. His request was turned down on a technicality that he probably viewed as a slight owing to his mestizo ancestry. At one point in the factional wars of the Spaniards, at least by the council's reconstruction of those events, Sebastián had acted in a way that appeared disloyal to the Crown; he had loaned a horse to Pizarro's brother at a time when the Pizarros were out of favor.

So Garcilaso lived a more modest life in Spain than he might have imagined when he left Peru. He lived with his father's brother, who was an old soldier and not well off. When his uncle died, along with other friends and protectors from the generation that remembered his father, his situation worsened. He considered going back to his homeland and at one point took steps to do so, but he feared that there was nothing to go back to. His choice was to be relatively poor and outcast in Spain or leave the claims to property and income that he had (and his writing projects as well) to go without office to a transformed Peru that he might no longer recognize.

Garcilaso's three major works—a scholarly annotated translation of León Hebreo's *Dialogues of Love* from Italian to Spanish, *The Florida of the Inca*, and *The Royal Commentaries of the Incas*—were written when Garcilaso was in his forties, fifties, and sixties, respectively. The works take Garcilaso and his readers successively closer and closer to the fundamental conflict that moved him to write in the first place: Europe's expansion made New World and Old World people aware of one another, creating problems for each people's understanding of itself and its place in the world. For Garcilaso this conflict was both external (in that he was discriminated against in Spain) and internal. His books were therapy for a brilliant and sensitive mind, but he probably never solved the problem to his satisfaction. Nor, for that matter, have we solved it, five centuries after Columbus landed.

Garcilaso de la Vega's simple answer to the dilemma of being caught between two worlds, belonging completely to neither, is given at the beginning of the first book of the *Royal Commentaries:*

> As experience has, since the discovery of the so-called New World, undeceived us about most of these doubts [concerning the makeup of the globe], we will pass them briefly by and go on to another part, whose conclusion I fear I shall never reach. But trusting in God's infinite

mercy, I will say at the outset that there is only one world, and although we speak of the Old World and the New, this is because the latter was lately discovered by us, and not because there are two.

For his readers and detractors who believed that there were two separate worlds, peopled by superior and inferior races, he adds darkly, "And to those who still imagine there are many [branches of humanity that are of different qualities], there is no answer except that they may remain in their heretical imaginings till they are undeceived in hell."

Works Cited and Suggestions for Further Reading

Vega, Garcilaso de la
1951   *The Florida of the Inca; A History of Adelantado, Hernando de Soto,*
        Governor and Captain General of the Kingdom of Florida. . . . Trans-
        lated and edited by John Grier Varner and Jeannette Johnson
        Varner. Austin: University of Texas Press.

Vega, Garcilaso de la
1966   *Royal Commentaries of the Incas, and General History of Peru.* Trans-
        lated with an introduction by Harold V. Livermore. Foreword by
        Arnold J. Toynbee. Austin: University of Texas Press.

Zárate, Agustín de
1967   *The Discovery and Conquest of Peru: A Translation of Books I to IV of*
        Agustín de Zarate's History of These Events, Supplemented by Eye-
        Witness Accounts of Certain Incidents . . . and . . . Later Historians.
        . . . Compiled and translated from the Spanish with an intro-
        duction by J. M. Cohen. Harmondsworth, UK: Penguin, 1968.

Pilgrim's Paradox

On December 22, 1881, Mark Twain addressed the Sons of New England in Philadelphia. "I rise to protest," he began. "I have kept still for years, but really I think there is no sufficient justification for this sort of thing. What do you want to celebrate those people for?—those ancestors of yours, of the Mayflower tribe, I mean." Mixing social critique with humor, Twain alluded to the Pilgrims' prejudices: "Your ancestors—yes, they were a hard lot; but, nevertheless, they gave us religious liberty to worship as they required us to worship, and political liberty to vote as the Church required." Portraying himself, as he often did, as a composite of the whole human race, "an infinitely shaded and exquisite mongrel," he asked, "Where are my ancestors? Whom shall I celebrate? Where shall I find the raw material? My first American ancestor . . . was an Indian; an early Indian; your ancestors skinned him alive, and I am an orphan."

Thanksgiving is a holiday built around a story: The Pilgrims, fleeing religious persecution, sailed from England to the New World aboard the *Mayflower*. They stepped ashore on Plymouth Rock and began a new colony. In unfamiliar territory, they came near starvation, but the Indian Squanto appeared and taught them to plant corn and make their living from the land. Led by William Bradford and Miles Standish, they survived these difficult early days, and when they brought in the first rich harvest, they set aside a day to give thanks to God for their good fortune. The chief Massasoit and their other Native American neighbors came bringing deer and wild turkeys, and together the Indians and the Pilgrims celebrated the first Thanksgiving.

The vague history (more myth, really) of the first Thanksgiving presents a scenario of the encounter of New World and Old World people that existed for only a moment, if it existed at all. It involves one of the least typical, and least successful, groups of European colonizers of the North American continent. Yet Thanksgiving is an important celebration throughout the United States, and like most things central to American culture, it is complicated and multilayered.

The historical trail of the first Thanksgiving begins (and practically ends) with a quotation from a letter by Edward Winslow written on December 11, 1621:

> Our harvest being gotten in, our Governour [William Bradford] sent foure men on fowling, that so we might after a more speciall manner rejoyce together, after we had gathered the fruit of our labours; they foure in one day killed as much fowls, as with a little helpe beside, served the Company almost a week, at which time amongst other Recreations, we exercised our Armes, many of the Indians coming amongst us, and amongst the rest their greatest King Massasoyt, with some nintie men, whom for three dayes we entertained and feasted, and they went out and killed five Deere, which they brought to the Plantation and bestowed on our Governour, and upon the Captains [Miles Standish], and others. And although it be not alwayes so plentiful as it was at this time with us, yet by the goodnesse of God, we are so farre from want, that we often with you partakes of our plentie. We have found the Indians very faithfull in their Covenant of Peace with us very loving and readie to pleasure us: we often goe to them, and they come to us some of us have bin fiftie myles by Land in the Country with them.

Even less is revealed in Bradford's *Of Plimoth Plantation*. He does not mention Massasoit's three-day visit or express any special sense of thanksgiving. In his notes from about September 1621, he simply says that "besides waterfowl there was a great store of wild turkeys, of which they took many, besides venison, etc. Besides they had about a peck a meal a week to a person, or now since harvest, Indian corn to that proportion."

The origin of Thanksgiving as a national holiday is even more ambiguous. In *The Fast and Thanksgiving Days of New England* (1895),

W. DeLoss Love records 696 New England observances of days of thanksgiving in the seventeenth century alone and laments the inadequacy of the archives. The dates fall nearly without pattern, on any day in any month. In 1879, the Reverend I. N. Tarbox looked for the origin of the holiday in his article, "Our New England Thanksgiving, Historically Considered." He concluded,

> The lesson to be learned from the survey thus made is, that Thanksgiving as we now have it, is the slow growth of many years. It did not come into the full strength of its existence in New England until after the close of the seventeenth century. For more than eighty years after the Pilgrims landed at Plymouth it was more or less miscellaneous in its order, and its times, and in its character.

Tarbox thought that the holiday had deeper Judeo-Christian roots, which he found in the Old Testament Feast of Tabernacles—"the feast of the harvest, the first fruits of thy labours, which thou has sown in the field; and the feast of in-gathering, which is in the end of the year when thou has gathered." The Bible instructed, "Ye shall rejoice before the Lord your God seven days."

George Washington declared February 19, 1795, to be a national Thanksgiving day, celebrating the suppression of the Whiskey Rebellion. He had proclaimed one earlier to mark the ratification of the Constitution, but both of these were onetime events. John Adams favored a more permanent holiday on May 9. Thomas Jefferson objected to the whole undertaking: Setting days of fasting and prayer was a religious matter, he argued, not the business of government. Many other Thanksgivings were proclaimed to observe a variety of military victories, but no regular national holiday was set. Throughout the early nineteenth century, a federal policy evolved of leaving the matter to the individual states.

Finally, after the battle of Gettysburg, Lincoln moved to proclaim a national day of Thanksgiving. Initially the holiday was set for August 6, but Sara Joseph Hale, editor of *Godey's Lady's Book,* and Secretary of State William Seward persuaded Lincoln to change the date to encompass the harvest festival traditions of many New England states. Lincoln proclaimed, "I do, therefore, invite my fellow citizens in every part of the United States . . . to set apart and observe the last Thursday of November next as a day of thanksgiving and praise to our beneficent Father who dwelleth in the heavens." Lincoln was building bridges and seeking to emphasize common traditions in "every part" of a nation splintered by war. Thanksgiving, an ambiguous, multipurpose holiday, was ideal for this purpose.

So the Pilgrims had little to do with the institutionalization of the present national holiday. And perhaps properly so. As colonists the Pilgrims were about the least successful on record if a colony's success is measured by growth. The people of Plymouth Colony were ultimately attracted to other, more dynamic centers, leaving their settlement and church, in Bradford's words, "like an ancient mother grown old, and forsaken of her children."

Kenneth Davies, in *The North Atlantic World in the Seventeenth Century* (1974), describes the Pilgrims' colonial enterprise bluntly, calling them "a settlement of exiles and drop-outs who entered a plantation covenant to walk in the same way. They had no royal charter, no authorizing act from a parent colony, no proprietorial sponsor, and no mercantile backing. They were squatters." Even Thoreau, in his *Cape Cod,* apologizes for the Pilgrims: "It must be confessed that the Pilgrims possessed but few of the qualities of the modern pioneer. They were not the ancestors of the American backwoodsmen."

And yet, the first Thanksgiving became the centerpiece of the national holiday. Perhaps this is because the story of the Pilgrims could be molded into a variety of forms, embellished and retold to make different points or emphasize different values or principles.

Daniel Webster saw the Pilgrims as the founders of a new and democratic political order based on religious principles. In his address on Forefathers' Day in 1820, he creatively rewrote the speech delivered on the Pilgrims' landing: "If God prosper us, we shall here begin a work which shall last for ages. We shall plant here a new society, in the principles of the fullest liberty, and the purest religion; . . . the temples of the true God shall rise, where now ascends the smoke of idolatrous sacrifice."

In the political interpretation of the story, the Pilgrims represent the seed of democracy in the New World. In this view, the Mayflower Compact—a modest and impromptu statement at best—is presented as the model and inspiration for later democratic charters, including the United States Constitution. It was actually a short and rather vague document that no modern lawyer would touch. It comprised only five sentences, the essence of which is that

[We] in the presence of God and one of another, covenant, and combine our selves together into a civill body politike, for our better ordering and preservation, and furtherance of the ends aforesaid; and by vertue hereof to enact, constitute, and frame such just and equall Lawes, Ordinances, acts, constitutions, offices from time to time, as shall be thought most meet and convenient for the generall good of the Colony: unto which we promise all due submission and obedience. (quoted in Winslow 1865)

The story of the Pilgrims has also been scripted as an epic romance, an early American version of Arthurian legend. Henry Wadsworth Longfellow's The *Courtship of Miles Standish* (1875) and Jane G. Austin's *Standish of Standish* (1889) develop the romantic theme. In her preface, Austin sets the tone for her heroic tale, which bears almost no relation to the recorded history of the Plymouth Colony: "I offer this story of Myles Standish, The Sword, the hero, who not for gain, not from necessity, not even from religious zeal, but purely in the knightly fervor of his blood, forsook home, and heritage, and glory, and ambition, to accompany that helpless band of exiles, and to be the Great-Heart of their Pilgrimage to the City that they sought."

Austin's is a melodramatic love story featuring Standish, John Alden, and Priscilla Moline. The Indians appear only briefly, announced by "The fiend is upon us!" and figuring as devious villains that Standish must overcome.

The story of the first Thanksgiving is also a parable about Indian-White relations. The late Lynn Ceci, an archeologist and ethnohistorian of the Northeast, in a fascinating article titled "Squanto and the Pilgrims" (her article prompted this essay), gently debunks the story that Squanto, the Indian guide and interpreter, taught the Pilgrims to fertilize their corn with fish (a practice that she found to be of European origin). Ceci proceeds to unravel large sections of the fabric of the first Thanksgiving story.

In particular, Ceci reveals Squanto to be a much more complex and interesting person than the "noble savage" often portrayed. The simplistic view of Squanto, like that of many Indians in European American folktales, was of a person with no history. He helped the Pilgrims because of his friendly nature. For example, in Wilma Pitchford Hays's 1958 story for children, "Paying for Indian Corn" "Squanto had learned a little English from fishermen whose ships had stopped in the New World."

In fact, Squanto had been kidnapped from Cape Cod and sold into slavery in Spain in 1614, six years before the Pilgrims sailed. He may have returned to Cape Cod a year later with Captain John Smith (if "Tantum" on Smith's manifest is Squanto), but in any case, he eventually made his way to England, where he lived with the treasurer of the Newfoundland Company. He then accompanied Captain John Mason to Newfoundland in 1617 (listed as "Tasquantum") and returned to England with Captain Thomas Dermer in 1618. Finally returning to New England with Dermer, he left the ship to rejoin his people, the Patuxet. Finding that none remained (all had been taken as slaves or had died of European diseases), he stayed with the Pilgrims as guide and interpreter.

According to Bradford, Squanto

> sought his own ends and played his own game, . . . putting the Indians in fear and drawing gifts from them to enrich himself, making them believe he could stir up war against whom he would, and make peace for whom he would. Yea, he made [the Indians] believe [the English] kept the plague buried in the ground, and could send it amongst whom they would, which did much to terrify the Indians and made them depend more on him, and seek more to him than to Massasoit.

In 1622, again according to Bradford, "Squanto fell sick of an Indian fever, bleeding much at the nose (which the Indians take for a symptom of death) and within a few days died there."

Ceci describes Squanto as an

> enterprising survivor and culture-broker who facilitated the meshing of disparate cultures on a new frontier. More importantly, the invented Squanto masks the more threatening and numerous Indians of the frontier period who, objecting to the usurpation and invasion of their lands, attacked and killed settlers—a more accurate representation but a history too uncomfortable for popular American consumption.

The historical archeologist James Deetz (1969) described the Pilgrims as more medieval than modern, "a culture as different from that of Americans today as are many cultures of modern Africa or Latin America." The feast of Thanksgiving celebrated in November is a phenomenon of our time, not theirs, a morality tale dealing with values central to modern American culture—religious freedom, self-reliance, political independence, and racial harmony.

At the end of his speech a century ago Mark Twain teased Philadelphia's society of the Sons of New England for making heroes of their Puritan ancestors:

> Hear me, I beseech you; get up an auction and sell Plymouth Rock! The pilgrims were a simple and ignorant race; they never had seen any good rocks before, or at least any that were not watched, and so they were excusable for hopping ashore in frantic delight and clapping an iron fence around this one. . . . Disband these societies, hotbeds of vice, of moral decay; perpetuators of ancestral superstition. Here on this board I see water. I see milk. I see the wild and deadly lemonade. These are but steps upon the downward path. Next we shall see tea, then chocolate, then coffee—hotel coffee. A few more years—all too few, I fear—mark my words, we shall have cider! Gentlemen pause ere it be too late.

Works Cited and Suggestions for Further Reading

Austin, Jane G.
1889   *Standish of Standish: A Story of the Pilgrims*. Boston: Riverside Press.

Bradford, William
1966 [1952]   *Of Plimoth Plantation, 1620–1647*. New York: Alfred A. Knopf.

Ceci, Lynn
1990   Squanto and the Pilgrims. *Society,* May-June 1990, v27, p40–44.

Davies, Kenneth
1974   *The North Atlantic World in the Seventeenth Century*. Minneapolis: University of Minnesota Press.

Deetz, James
1969   The Reality of the Pilgrim Fathers. *Natural History*, November 1969, p32–45.

Ellison, Richard
1988   Who Were the Pilgrims? *New England Monthly*, November 1988, p69–119.

Hayes, Wilma Pitchford
1958   Paying for Indian Corn. *Jack and Jill*.

Longfellow, Henry Wadsworth
1875   *The Courtship of Miles Standish*. New York: E. P. Dutton.

Love, W. DeLoss
1895   *The Fast and Thanksgiving Days of New England*. Boston: Riverside
        Press.

Tarbox, I. N.
1879   Our New England Thanksgiving, Historically Considered. *The New
        Englander*, March 1879, p249–252.

Thoreau, Henry David
1865   *Cape Cod*. Boston: Ticknor & Fields.

Twain, Mark
1881   Address to the New England Sons. *The New York Times,* December
        26, 1881, p2.

Webster, Daniel
1985 [1820]   *A Discourse, Delivered at Plymouth, December 22, 1820.*
               Woodbridge, CT: Research Publications, 1985 (reprint
               edition).

Winslow, Edward
1865   *Mourt's Relation or Journal of the Plantation at Plymouth.* Introduction
        and notes by Henry Martyn Dexter. Boston: J. K. Wiggin.

Encountering
the
European
World

his section includes the stories of two coincidental dis-
coveries. In both cases two groups came to a place at
about the same time. In the earlier of these two coincidences, Inuit people, circling the Arctic from the Bering
Straits across northern Canada, came to Greenland at
about the same time that Norse sailors came to the island from the
east. They met at the southern tip of the island. A partnership between the two groups never really emerged; the northern Europeans'
economy was not well suited to Greenland and they never adopted
enough of the Inuit way of life to make their settlement a long-term
success. After four centuries, the Norse Greenlanders' colony failed.

The other coincidence was a near miss that occurred when a great
fleet of ships from Ming China was sent out to visit the ports of the
Indian Ocean in the fifteenth century. China was the most powerful
state in the world at the time and it was making a statement of that
fact through these sponsored voyages. Its great fleet sailed down the
east coast of Africa as far as Madagascar and brought back tribute and
emissaries from African and Asian kingdoms. It also brought a giraffe
back to the Chinese capital. The Chinese delegation did not, however, meet the Portuguese explorers who were at about the same time
exploring the west coast of Africa. Neither Europe nor China had ever
sent explorers by sea so far into unknown territory, yet they were just
a few years' time and a few days' sailing from running into one
another.

Had China and Europe developed a relationship at this time, the
events described in "Coffee, Tea, or Opium?" might have been very
different. The Opium Wars of the 1840s took place 400 years after the
Ming Fleet sailed, and in that conflict the English used sea power to
force the Chinese to allow the foreigners to bring opium into the
country. The degree of mutual ignorance and misunderstanding between the English and Chinese was as great in the nineteenth century as it had been centuries earlier between the Spanish and the
Aztecs. In the period since the Opium Wars, the global practice of for-

eign policy, international trade, and the management of trade deficits has never been the same.

The encounter between the people of Europe and East Asia has been going on far longer than that between Europe and the Americas. Marco Polo's accounts and those of other travelers provided the motivation for Columbus and others to sail west in the first place. The protracted Europe-Asia encounter perhaps lacks some of the drama of great voyages of discovery and unknown worlds, but the significance of this interaction for our world is unsurpassed. This interaction may also be characterized as a contact period that is still under way. The chapter describing the Chinese monk Tripitaka's journey to the west in search of Buddhist scripture provides an early record of the fact that exploration beyond national and cultural boundaries was always important. Long before there were easy or fast means of transportation, people traveled great distances in search of knowledge about the world and other people. It is a part of our nature.

The Emperor's Giraffe

A huge fleet left port in 1414 and sailed westward on a voyage of trade and exploration. The undertaking far surpassed anything Columbus, Isabela, and Ferdinand could have envisioned. The fleet included at least sixty-two massive trading galleons, any of which could have held Columbus's three small ships on its decks. The largest galleons were more than 400 feet long and 150 feet wide (the *Santa María,* Columbus's largest vessel, was about 90 by 30 feet), and each could carry about 1,500 tons (Columbus's ships combined could carry about 400 tons). More than 100 smaller vessels accompanied the galleons. All told, 30,000 people went on the voyage, compared with Columbus's crew of ninety-some.

The commander's name was Zheng He (Cheng Ho), the Grand Eunuch of the Three Treasures and the most acclaimed admiral of the Ming dynasty. He was sailing from the South China Sea across the Indian Ocean, heading for the Persian Gulf and Africa. As the historian Philip Snow notes in his wonderful book *The Star Raft* (1988), "Zheng He was the Chinese Columbus. He has become for China, as Columbus has for the West, the personification of maritime endeavour." The flotilla was called the star raft after the luminous presence of the emperor's ambassadors onboard.

Zheng He did not really set out to explore unknown lands—neither did Columbus, for that matter—for the Chinese were aware of most of the countries surrounding the Indian Ocean. For centuries, China had been a principal producer and consumer of goods moving east and west from Mediterranean, African, and Middle Eastern trading centers. With this trade came cultural and ideological exchange.

121

Detail of The Tribute Giraffe with Attendant, *by Shen Tu, Ming Dynasty; Philadelphia Museum of Art, given by John T. Dorrance.*

Zheng He, like many Chinese of his time, was a Muslim, and his father and his father's father before him had made the pilgrimage to Mecca. But in Zheng He's day, the trade routes were controlled by Arabian, Persian, and Indian merchants. Private Chinese traders had been barred from traveling to the west for several centuries. China had been conquered by Genghis Khan and his descendants in the 1200s, and the Mongol emperors of the subsequent Yuan dynasty were the first to impose these constraints. In 1368, the Chinese expelled the Mongol rulers and established the Ming dynasty, which was destined to rule for the next 300 years. (Thus, in 1492 Columbus was searching for a "Gran Khan" who had been put out of business 124 years earlier.) After the period of Mongol rule, China became strongly isolationist, placing even more severe restrictions on Chinese traders. In 1402, an outward-looking emperor named Yong'le (Yung-lo) came to power. Seeking to reassert a Chinese presence on the western seas and to enhance the prestige of his rule and dynasty, he began funding spectacular voyages by Zheng He. As the sociologist Janet Abu-Lughod notes in *Before European Hegemony* (1989), "The impressive show of force that paraded around the Indian Ocean during the first three decades of the fifteenth century was intended to signal the 'barbarian nations' that China had reassumed her rightful place in the firmament of nations—had once again become the 'Middle Kingdom' of the world."

As Zheng He pressed westward in 1414, he sent part of the fleet north to Bengal, and there the Chinese travelers saw a wondrous creature. None like it had ever been seen in China, although it was not completely unheard of. In 1225, Zhao Rugua, a customs inspector at the city of Quanzhou, had recorded a secondhand description of such a beast in his strange and wonderful *Gazetteer of Foreigners*. He said it had a leopard's hide, a cow's hoofs, a ten-foot-tall body, and a nine-foot neck towering above that. He called it a *zula*, possibly a corruption of *zurafa*, the Arabic word for giraffe.

The giraffe the travelers saw in Bengal was already more than 5,000 miles from home. It had been brought there as a gift from the ruler of the prosperous African city-state of Malindi, one of several trading centers lining the east coast of Africa (Malindi is midway along modern Kenya's coast, three degrees south of the equator). Zheng He's diplomats persuaded the Bengal king to offer the animal as a gift to the Chinese emperor. They also persuaded the Malindi ambassadors to send home for another giraffe. When Zheng He returned to Beijing, he was able to present the emperor with two of the exotic beasts.

A pair of giraffes in Beijing in 1415 was well worth the cost of the expedition. The Chinese thought the giraffe (despite its having one horn too many) was a unicorn (*ch'i-lin*), whose arrival, according to Confucian tradition, meant that a sage of the utmost wisdom and benevolence was in their presence. It was a great gift, therefore, to bring to the ambitious ruler of a young dynasty. The giraffes were presented to the emperor Yong'le by exotic envoys from the kingdom of Malindi, whom the Chinese treated royally. They and their marvelous gift so excited China's curiosity about Africa that Zheng He sent word to the kingdom of Mogadishu (then one of the most powerful trading states in East Africa and now the capital of modern Somalia) and to other African states, inviting them to send ambassadors to the Ming emperor.

The response of the African rulers was overwhelmingly generous, for China and Africa had been distant trading partners from the time of the Han dynasty (206 BC to AD 220). In the *Universal Christian Topography,* written about AD 525 by Kosmas, a Byzantine monk known as the "Indian Traveler," Sri Lanka is described as a trading center frequented by both Chinese and Africans. Envoys from a place called Zengdan—the name translates as "Land of Blacks"—visited China several times in the eleventh century. And a Chinese map compiled in the early fourteenth century shows Madagascar and the southern tip of Africa in remarkable detail, nearly two centuries before the Portuguese "discovered" the Cape of Good Hope. Archeologists find china (why the English word came to be synonymous with glazed pottery and porcelain, instead of silk or spices, is unclear) from the Han and later dynasties all along the east coast of Africa.

The African emissaries to the Ming throne came with fabulous gifts, including objects for which entrepreneurs had long before managed to create a market in the Far East—tortoiseshell, elephant ivory, and rhinoceros-horn medicine. On their many visits they also brought zebras, ostriches, and other exotica. In return, the Ming court sent gold, spices, silk, and other presents. Zheng He was sent with his fleet of great ships on yet another voyage across the Indian Ocean to accompany some of the foreign emissaries home. This escort was the first of several imperially supported trips to Africa. According to official records, they went to Mogadishu, Brava, and perhaps Malindi; Snow (in *The Star Raft*) suggests that these Chinese expeditions may have gone still farther—to Zanzibar, Madagascar, and southern Africa.

Meanwhile, as the Chinese were pushing down the east coast of Africa, Portuguese mariners were tentatively exploring the west coast. They had started the process in the early fifteenth century and were steadily working their way south. Bartolomeu Dias reached the Cape of Good Hope in 1488 and was the first of these mariners to see the Indian Ocean. Surely the Europeans and Chinese were poised to meet somewhere in southern Africa, where perhaps they would have set up trading depots for their mutual benefit.

This did not happen, however. Emperor Yong'le died in 1424, and by 1433 the Ming dynasty discontinued its efforts to secure tributary states and trading partners around the Indian Ocean. In Beijing, those favoring an isolationist foreign policy won out, and the massive funding needed to support Zheng He's fleet—difficult to sustain during what was a period of economic decline in China—was canceled. As Edwin Reischauer and John Fairbank note in *East Asia: The Great Tradition* (1958),

> The voyages must be regarded as a spectacular demonstration of the capacity of early Ming China for maritime expansion, made all the more dramatic by the fact that Chinese ideas of government and official policies were fundamentally indifferent, if not actually opposed, to such an expansion. This contrast between capacity and performance, as viewed in retrospect from the vantage point of our modern world of trade and overseas expansion, is truly striking.

The contrast also refutes the argument that as soon as a country possesses the technology of overseas trade and conquest it will use it. Zheng He's fleet was 250 times the size of Columbus's, and the Ming navy was many times larger and more powerful than the combined maritime strength of all of Europe. Yet China perceived its greatest challenges and opportunities to be internal ones, and Yong'le's overseas agenda was forgotten. Restrictions on private trade were reimposed, and commercial and military ventures in the Indian Ocean and South China Sea in subsequent centuries were dominated by the Portuguese, Arabs, Indians, Spaniards, Japanese, Dutch, British, and Americans. Zheng He's magnificent ships finally rotted at their moorings.

Works Cited and Suggestions for Further Reading

Abu-Lughod, Janet L.
1989   *Before European Hegemony: The World System* A.D. *1250–1350.* New
        York: Oxford University Press.

McCrindle, John W. (ed. and compiler)
1979 [1901]   *Ancient India as Described in Classical Literature: Being a Col-
                lection of Greek and Latin Texts Relating to India, Extracted
                from Herodotus, Strabo, Plinius, Aelianus, Kosmas, Barde
                sanes, Porphyrios, Strobaios, Dion Chrysostom, Dionysios,
                Philostratos, Nonnos, Diodorus Siculus, the Itinerary and Ro-
                mance History of Alexander and Other Works. . . .* New
                Delhi: Oriental Books Reprint Corp.

Reischauer, Edwin O., and John K. Fairbank
1958   *East Asia: The Great Tradition.* Boston: Houghton Mifflin.

Snow, Philip
1988   *The Star Raft: China's Encounter with Africa.* London: Weidenfeld &
        Nicolson.

Coffee, Tea, or Opium?

In 1839, China's commissioner for foreign trade, Lin Zexu (Lin Tse-hsu), was running out of diplomatic options. Traders from the East India Company and other European enterprises were pressing him ever more forcefully to turn a blind eye to the illegal importation of opium into his country. They were implicitly backed by Britain's heavily armored warships—such as the *Blenheim* and *Wellesley*, carrying seventy-four cannons each—which could crush China's navy and lay waste to her ports. But the opium trade was damaging public health and bleeding China of its wealth. In 1838, the Manchu emperor had given Lin extensive power and ordered him to control the demand of China's people for opium and force the barbarian merchants to cut off the supply.

After his appointment, Lin began to study European culture, looking for clues to barbarian behavior. He obtained a partial translation of Emer de Vattel's 1758 *Le Droit des Gens* ("The Law of Nations"), and he bought and studied the British ship *Cambridge*. Although it was not the largest of the "East Indiamen"—big defended freighters—and although it had been stripped of its guns and its intricate rigging was a mystery to Lin's sailors, the ship was ample evidence that these British were clever at naval warfare.

Lin also visited Macao, the Portuguese trading entrepôt near Canton, and carried out some anthropological fieldwork:

As soon as I entered the wall of Macao, a hundred barbarian soldiers dressed in barbarian military uniform, led by the barbarian headman, greeted me. They marched in front of my sedan playing barbarian music and led me into the city. . . . On this day, everyone man and woman, came out on the street or leaned from the window to take a look. Unfortunately the barbarian costume was too absurd. The men, their bodies wrapped tightly in short coats and long "legs," resembled in shape foxes and rabbits as impersonated in the plays. . . . Their beards, with abundant whiskers, were half shaved off and only a piece was kept. Looking at them all of a sudden was frightening. That the Cantonese referred to them as "devils" was indeed not vicious disparagement. (quoted in Chang 1964)

Although the Chinese forbade opium importation, willing trading partners were easily found among the Chinese merchants. And if trade became too difficult for the foreigners in the principal port of Canton, there were a thousand miles of coastline, and thousands of miles more of inland borders, through which opium could be transported. Lin saw that the opium trade was ruining China. Informed by his reading of de Vattel and by his extensive dealings with the British representatives, in early 1839 he appealed to Queen Victoria, attempting to conceal the sense of superiority that the Chinese rulers felt toward Westerners:

We have heard that in your honorable nation, too, the people are not permitted to smoke [opium], and that offenders in this particular expose themselves to sure punishment. . . . Though not making use of it one's self, to venture nevertheless to manufacture and sell it, and with it to seduce the simple folk of this land, is to seek one's own livelihood by exposing others to death, to seek one's own advantage by other men's injury. Such acts are bitterly abhorrent to the nature of man and are utterly opposed to the ways of heaven. . . . We now wish to find, in cooperation with your honorable sovereignty, some means of bringing to a perpetual end this opium, so hurtful to mankind: we in this land forbidding the use of it, and you, in the nations of your dominion, forbidding its manufacture. (quoted in Chang 1964)

The British were the biggest traders in China, but merchants from the United States were present too. Lin considered petitioning this other, possibly significant state, but understood that twenty-four chiefs governed the American people (the individual states' governors), and thought that communicating with them all would be too difficult.

In his letter to Queen Victoria, Lin sought to explain the situation logically. Earlier communications from the Chinese government had not been so diplomatic. The commander of Canton had sent an edict to the Western traders demanding, "Could your various countries stand one day without trading with China?" This threat came in part from the Chinese leaders' delusion that the British would die if deprived of tea, China's largest export (a delusion the British may have shared). The same edict took note that, according to the Western press, "Your motives are to deplete the Middle Kingdom's wealth and destroy the lives of the Chinese people. There is no need to dwell on the topic that the wealth of the Celestial Empire, where all five metals are produced and precious deposits abound, could not be exhausted by such a mere trifle, but for what enmity do you want to kill the Chinese people?"

China had withstood barbarian traders without difficulty for 2,000 years. But now it was feeling the aftershock of the Western encounter with the Americas and with the closely related expansion of European influence across the globe. The importation of opium reached staggering proportions in the early nineteenth century after the British-run East India Company took control of the drug's production in India. During the trading season of 1816–1817, about 4,600 150-pound chests of opium entered China. This number rose to 22,000 by 1831–1832 and 35,000 by 1837–1838. That was more than 5.25 million pounds of opium, the carefully collected and dried sap extruded from 4.8 trillion opium poppies.

The period from the seventeenth century to the present could be termed the Age of Addiction, for the international economy and the fortunes of nations depended on trade in addictive or semiaddictive agricultural products. The young United States exported tobacco, the habit for which spread rapidly across Europe, Africa, and Asia. The Spaniards carried the New World practice of tobacco smoking to Europe and the East Indies, and as its popularity spread, the plant came to be widely cultivated throughout the Old World. In their Indonesian colonies the Dutch tried filling their pipes with a combination of opium and tobacco. The Chinese continued to smoke the opium, but left out the tobacco. The British became addicted to the carefully processed leaves of *Camellia sinensis,* or Chinese tea (originally, China was the only exporter). Caffeine-rich coffee was another drug for which Europeans and others developed a craving. A native plant of

Ethiopia, coffee's range of cultivation expanded hand in hand with European colonialism. Perfect growing conditions were found in both the New World and Southeast Asia, giving rise to the exotic names for coffee familiar today: Jamaica Blue Mountain, Mocha Java, Guatemalan, Sumatran, and Colombian. These and other nonessential but deeply desired plant products—cocaine, chocolate, and marijuana—have captured huge markets.

Addictive substances are wonderful exports for the countries that produce and ship them. They are highly valuable and compact agricultural products that can be exchanged for hard currency, and the demand of addicts is—for physiological reasons—what economists would call "highly inelastic." Addicts will do almost anything to get a fix. Farmers get much more from their land and effort than they would by growing products for a local market, and middlemen on both sides of the border get rich. The losers in the transaction—apart from the users themselves—are the importing countries, which run up uncontrollable trade deficits.

From the opening of the Silk Road in the Middle Ages, Western countries were eager to obtain Chinese spices, fabrics, and tea, viewing them as superior to European products. The problem for England and other nations was that they had very little that China wanted, so they had to pay in the most respected and accepted international currency, Spanish silver dollars. With good reason, the Chinese thought the British could not live without tea. About all China would take in trade was British woolen and cotton cloth. American merchants, lacking England's textile manufacturing infrastructure, struggled still more to find anything the Chinese would take in trade. They too paid mainly with Spanish silver, but they also brought natural products—sealskins and other furs from the Northwest Coast, aromatic wood, cotton, wild American ginseng—with which to trade.

By capitalizing on a massive addiction to smoked opium in China—and in substantial measure helping to create it—England and the other Western nations shifted the balance of trade in their favor. As the social historian Fernand Braudel put it, "China was now literally being paid in smoke (and what smoke!)." Most of the rest of what England traded was woven cotton, also grown and spun in India. In return, at the time of Commissioner Lin's appeal to Queen Victoria, the Chinese were trading about 60 percent tea; 12 percent silks; and most of the rest, about 25 percent, silver and gold.

The opium trade was not the only alarming foreign influence in Lin's day. The barbarians seemed to have designs on Chinese territory. The port of Canton lay thirty miles upriver from the great Gulf of Canton, twenty miles wide and fifty miles long. At the western approach to the bay was the Portuguese trading colony of Macao, which the Chinese had allowed to exist since 1557. On the other side of the gulf lay the island of Hong Kong, which the British sought to turn into a secure headquarters for their trading operations. Even if the Europeans had lacked naval superiority, they could have defended both places from invasion by land or sea. China had always insisted that barbarians of any stripe carry out their trade and then leave, but instead of acting as temporary visitors, the Western traders were staying longer and longer, becoming in effect permanent residents.

Another major grievance was that the foreigners would not submit to Chinese laws when in China. Some European sailors murdered Chinese citizens, but their leaders would not turn over the culprits to the Chinese magistrates. Lin's research revealed that foreigners in England were required to obey British law, but when he confronted the British commanders with this double standard, they merely conceded that he had a case and again refused to turn over British subjects to almost certain execution. Other European and American traders acted similarly.

Despite the barbarian offenses, Lin preferred negotiation and reasoned discussion to fighting a battle that he felt would be difficult to win. In a final, carefully worded letter to Queen Victoria, he wrote,

> Let us suppose that foreigners came from another country and brought opium into England, and seduced the people of your country to smoke it. Would not you, the sovereign of the said country, look upon such a procedure with anger, and in your just indignation endeavor to get rid of it? Now we have always heard that Your Highness possesses a most kind and benevolent heart. Surely then you are incapable of doing or causing to be done unto another that which you should not wish another to do unto you. (quoted in Chang 1964)

Unfortunately for Commissioner Lin, moral persuasion has not, historically, proved very effective in dealing with drug smuggling or rulers who sanction it. Unofficially, the contents of the letter were probably widely known but, as with his previous attempts, Lin received no official response. Britain was determined that the opium trade would continue, by force if necessary, and because China had been unwilling to open formal diplomatic channels, the British government would not accept a letter to the queen from a commissioner.

Lin's efforts to rein in the barbarians and subdue the Chinese appetite for opium were ultimately unsuccessful, and the emperor harshly accused him of failing: "Externally you wanted to stop the trade, but it has not been stopped. Internally you wanted to wipe out the outlaws, but they are not cleared away. . . . You are just making excuses with empty words. Nothing has been accomplished but many troubles have been created. Thinking of these things I cannot contain my rage. What do you have to say now?"

Lin replied that the Chinese should address the threat and fight the British, falling back to the interior and fighting a guerrilla war if necessary. He warned the emperor not to attempt to placate the British: "The more they get the more they demand, and if we do not overcome them by force of arms there will be no end to our troubles. Moreover there is every probability that if the English are not dealt with, other foreigners will soon begin to copy and even outdo them."

In June 1839, Lin had 20,000 chests of opium destroyed in Canton, and the foreign merchants fell back to Macao. The British sent a fleet of their most powerful warships on a punitive expedition, and they overwhelmed the Chinese fleet whenever they faced it. Among their warships were the "ships-of-the-line," massively armed vessels that demonstrated the advantage of superior technology over superior numbers in modern warfare. In the summer of 1842, China was forced to sign the humiliating Treaty of Nanking, which required $21 million in reparations; opened five ports to British trade (including Canton and Shanghai); and ceded Hong Kong, surrounding islands, and part of the mainland to Queen Victoria. China also agreed that future Chinese-British relations would be on terms of "complete equality." This condition seems ironic, because the terms of the treaty were certainly in the Western merchants' favor. This wording was insisted upon by the British, however, because previously China had dealt with Westerners as barbarian traders, never recognizing them as official representatives of foreign governments. Nowhere did the treaty mention opium, but everyone knew that the drug had been at the heart of the war.

One hundred fifty years later, China still feels the sting of this defeat. The treaty providing for the return of Hong Kong in 1997 was viewed as just a fraction of the restitution owed. In 1990, writing in the *Beijing Review,* the historian Hu Sheng, president of the Chinese Academy of Social Sciences, lamented the cost of the war in Chinese health, hard currency, and national honor. He also observed that for the next hundred years China was under continuous attack by the West and Japan, but because the emperors were willing to tolerate their presence, the people were unable to rise up and throw out the foreigners. In his view, and in that of many Chinese, "Only the Chinese Communist Party could do this."

For his failure to curb the barbarians, Lin Zexu was demoted and disgraced, and spent the last few years before his death supervising irrigation projects and the repair of dikes. In retrospect, he is regarded as a hero. "The Chinese army, commanded by Lin," writes Hu, "resisted the invaders together with the local people. However, the corrupt Qing court was unable to continue the resistance and succumbed to the invaders."

Commissioner Lin would no doubt feel vindicated, and perhaps even take some pleasure, in the way many Western nations are now on the receiving end of the drug policies they helped invent.

Works Cited and Suggestions for Further Reading

Chang Hsin-pao
1964   *Commissioner Lin and the Opium War.* Cambridge, MA: Harvard University Press.

Cunynghame, Arthur Augustus Thurlow, Sir
1845   *The Opium War: Being Recollections of Service in China.* Philadelphia: G. B. Zieber.

Fay, Peter Ward
1975   *The Opium War, 1840–1842: Barbarians in the Celestial Empire in the Early Part of the Nineteenth Century and the War by Which They Forced Her Gates Ajar.* New York: Norton.

Latimer, Dean, and Jeff Goldberg
1981   *Flowers in the Blood.* New York: Franklin Watts.

Waley, Arthur
1979   *The Opium War Through Chinese Eyes.* Stanford: Stanford University Press.

Walker, William O.
1991   *Opium and Foreign Policy.* Chapel Hill: University of North Carolina Press.

Tripitaka's Journey to the West

In A.D. 629, the Buddhist monk Hsüan-tsang (Xuanzang) defied imperial law and set out alone from China, heading for the west. His destination was India, the Buddha's homeland, and he sought to bring back sacred texts concerning the Buddha's teaching and its interpretations. In China it was a time of Buddhist revival; recent emperors had embraced Buddhism, and for Buddhist monks and believers, conditions were something like those that existed in Rome after the emperor Constantine converted to Christianity. Hsüan-tsang was frustrated, however, because the great Buddhist texts available revealed only a part of Buddhist doctrine. The texts that the Chinese monks had contradicted themselves and did not answer the question that troubled Hsüan-tsang the most: Could only some humans attain enlightenment, or could all? This and other philosophical questions, and the fragmentary collection of texts available to him and his fellow monks, moved Hsüan-tsang to journey to the west, to the land of the Buddha, to collect sacred writings and bring them back.

The historical figure Hsüan-tsang has come to be known by the honorific name "Tripitaka" (which means "basket," and also is a name for the three major divisions of the Buddhist sacred literature), and his journey to the west played an important role in the emergence of Buddhism as a powerful religion in China and Japan. His journey came at the beginning the T'ang dynasty (618–907), which has been called the "golden age" of Buddhism in China.

As the anthropologist Mary Helms notes in her fascinating book *Ulysses' Sail: An Ethnographic Odyssey of Power, Knowledge, and Geographical Distance* (1988), the traditional anthropological approach to long-distance contact between people has been to look at trade. Especially for archaeologists, whose domain covers most of the human past, contact between widely separated groups is inferred from finding the artifacts of one group among the archaeological remains of the other. This is not the only kind of interaction that ancient people (or modern) have with distant groups, and Tripitaka's pilgrimage in search of Buddhist texts is an example. Helms looks at these less tangible effects of long-distance contact, the kinds like Tripitaka's that spread "esoteric knowledge" with ideological and political significance. This kind of contact does not always leave obvious archaeological traces, but is surely important and has been going on since we evolved as a species.

In the seventh century, the odds were not particularly good that a single person might travel safely through thousands of miles of central Eurasia, which at the time was divided into hundreds of small and competitive states. The story of Hsüan-tsang's journey is from beginning to end full of confrontations with bandits and highwaymen (and a great many demons and malevolent spirits). On the first day of the trip, as an example, he accepted the services of a Central Asian guide named Banda; Banda showed up nearly a day late with a wizened old man in tow, riding an equally wizened old horse. Undaunted, Hsüan-tsang traded his fine horse (for he came from a family of some wealth and status) for the man's bony old mount because a fortune-teller had told him he would leave China on a skinny roan horse. That night, while pretending to be asleep, the monk saw Banda creeping toward him with a knife, but in the first of Hsüan-tsang's many miraculous close calls on the trip, Banda turned around and went back to sleep without harming the monk. Hsüan-tsang left Banda the next day. He then set out alone to cross the desert of Hami and found himself confronted with unearthly apparitions of desert barbarians who disappeared into the sand as he approached. A voice from the sky said, "Do not be afraid," and as happens throughout the accounts of his journey, he was saved by divine aid.

Finding historical accuracy in the accounts of Hsüan-tsang's trip is very difficult. The story has become a classic text in Chinese literature. Perhaps the most widely known retelling was by the sixteenth-century poet Wu Ch'eng-en in a novel called *Hsi-yü chi,* or "Monkey." In this allegorical version a magical monkey guides Hsüan-tsang to the west to collect his three baskets of Buddhist scripture. The *Hsi-yü chi* is wonderfully translated and annotated in the three-volume *Journey to the West,* by Anthony C. Yu (Chicago University Press, 1977). The fifteenth-century story may have combined other travelers' accounts, since Hsüan-tsang was not the only Chinese pilgrim to visit India. More than forty Chinese Buddhists (and also some Korean monks) had gone before, with the earliest recorded pilgrimages being around AD 260.

Hsüan-tsang lived at a critical time in China's history. In the late sixth and early seventh centuries AD, China was in the midst of climactic social, political, and philosophical struggles. Then as now, China was a mosaic of diverse peoples with different languages, religions, and ideas about political autonomy. More than eight centuries before, in 221 BC, Shi Huangdi had managed to bring the diverse parts of China under imperial rule. He was the great unifier of China whose tomb is guarded by the famous legions of terra-cotta soldiers that have recently been excavated. Shi Huangdi's Qin dynasty enforced uniformity in the written language and currency, and even regulated the widths of the axles of vehicles so that all roads would be passable (especially for the imperial army, which was not made of terra-cotta and spent considerable effort marching around China subjugating stubborn petty kings). He also tried to unify China's ideology by burning books of questionable doctrine.

Between the Qin unification and Hsüan-tsang's time, however, political fragmentation had been the rule. For three hundred years before Hsüan-tsang's birth in AD 596, China had been divided into many small kingdoms. In AD 581 the Sui dynasty, led by Sui Wên-ti, seized power and again unified China's diverse regions and subcultures. The Sui emperors reorganized the empire's economy and laws, and sought cultural common ground by embracing Confucianism, Taoism, and Buddhism. The Sui dynasty lasted only forty years, and in fact fell before Hsüan-tsang left for India, but it laid the groundwork for the powerful T'ang dynasty that followed it, and indeed for modern China.

Hsüan-tsang's journey became not so much a solitary march through hostile lands as a series of state visits from court to court and monastery to monastery. He was a masterful teacher and debater of

Buddhist doctrine, and his reputation preceded him wherever he went in India. Soon his problems were not only with bandits, but with competing rulers who wanted to have this famous and exotic Chinese monk in their courts. At Turfan, the first kingdom he encountered, he had to stage a three-day hunger strike to be allowed to leave, and then only with the promise that he would stay three years on his return trip (but by then he found that the Turfan kingdom no longer existed, having been annexed by China). Although he was a foreigner, Hsüan-tsang was something of a Buddhist missionary in the land where Buddha had lived (Siddhartha Gautama, the Buddha, lived about 560–480 BC, and so died more than 1,100 years before Hsüan-tsang went to India).

Like China before the Sui unification, India was composed of many kingdoms, and like India today, it was a land of many religions, with Hinduism, Jainism, and Buddhism being the dominant ones. Two of India's most powerful modern religions, Sikhism and Islam, were not in practice during Hsüan-tsang's travels: Islam arose from the teachings of the prophet Mohammed, who lived from c. 570 to 632 and was thus a contemporary of Hsüan-tsang. Sikhism, a monotheistic religion that emerged in the sixteenth century, incorporated aspects of Islam and Hinduism in a body of teaching that rejected the caste system and the worship of idols.

Hsüan-tsang had two other notable contemporaries, who played dominant roles in reshaping religions on both the eastern and western ends of Eurasia, in Japan and Europe. Pope Gregory I (AD 540–604) was an early Christian pope who shaped the papacy as a commanding social, philosophical, and political force during Europe's medieval period. Using the revenues from the church's large estates, he supported missionary work. He directed Saint Augustine of Canterbury to go to England and liberally combine Christian teaching with local pagan religions. As well as being known for Gregorian chants, Gregory I helped bring about the conversion of England.

The other influential Hsüan-tsang contemporary was the Japanese prince Shotoku (593–621), who acted as regent to his aunt the empress. He opened official channels of communication with China and borrowed extensively from Chinese imperial policies in strengthening the authority of the central government in Japan. He also promoted the spread of Buddhism in Japan, building and supporting many temples. In the century that followed, Buddhism came to be a central part of the aristocratic ideology.

During his long journey to the west, Hsüan-tsang debated with Hindu and Jain philosophers and sought to convince Indian princes of the logical superiority of Buddhist doctrine. The high point of Hsüan-tsang's trip was his more than five-year stay at the great monastery of Nālandā. Sīlabhadra, the famous monk of the Idealist school of Buddhism, lived and taught there. Hsüan-tsang was welcomed by the 10,000 monks of the monastery and was taken to greet this great master. According to Arthur Waley (1952), "Twenty responsible, middle-aged monks had coached him in the etiquette to be observed on such an occasion. They brought him in into the presence of the aged Sīlabhadra. . . . As became a would-be disciple he crawled towards Sīlabhadra on his elbows and knees, clacking his feet together and bumping his head on the ground."

Tripitaka explained that he had come from China to study and take back to China the *Yoga Sāstra,* the sacred text most relevant to Idealist Buddhism.

> Sīlabhadra turned to his nephew Buddhabhadra, a man of over seventy, and said, "Tell them about that dream I had three years ago." The gist of Sīlabhadra's dream was that three mysterious figures had appeared to him when he lay asleep at night, telling him that through his agency the true doctrine of the *Yoga Sāstra* was to be spread among peoples who as yet knew nothing of it. "In due time," they said, "a monk will come from China, desirous to understand the Great Law and wishing you to teach it to him. So be on the look-out for him."

Hsüan-tsang had traveled perhaps 5,000 miles already, having crossed Asia north of the Himalayas, coming through the Hindu Kush into modern Afghanistan, Pakistan, and Kashmir. Now, having crossed the kingdoms of central India, he had reached the lands in which the Buddha had lived more than a millennium before. In the lands around the monastery of Nālandā, he visited the famous shrines of the Buddha's life, including the Vulture Peak, where Buddha had preached the Lotus Sutra. The epic *Journey to the West* begins,

> *The rich T'ang ruler issued a decree,*
> *Deputing Hsüan-tsang to seek the source of Zen.*
> *He bent his mind to find the Dragon Den,*

Firmly resolved to climb the Vulture Peak.
Through how many states did he roam beyond his own?
Through clouds and hills he passed ten thousand times.
He now leaves the Throne to go to the West;
He'll keep law and faith to reach the Great Void.

Hsüan-tsang/Tripitaka worked long years at Nālandā, studying and discussing the *Yogā-cārya-bhūmi śāstra,* the foundation text of the Idealist school of Buddhism. Gradually, however, his desire to return his knowledge to China, and to spend the rest of his years translating the many texts he had acquired, overcame his desire to study at Nālandā. One day a monk named Vajra, who studied Jainism, walked unannounced into Hsüan-tsang's room. Hsüan-tsang said,

> I am a Chinese monk. I have been studying in India for many years and should now like to go home. Please consult your omens [for Jains were known for accurate fortune-telling] and tell me whether I shall get back safely, and also whether I ought to start at once or stay a little longer. I should also like to know how much longer I am going to live.

After consulting the omens, the Jain monk said,

> The omens are favourable to your staying on, and if you do so you will win respect among religious and laymen everywhere in India. If you go, you will get back safely and continue to be greatly respected here, only not to the same extent as if you stay on. Your natural span of life ceases after ten years, but a fresh stock of blessing earned in the future, might considerably extend it.

A fresh stock of blessing presumably did come to Hsüan-tsang, for he lived many more than the ten foretold by the Jain. He also made it back to China, carrying a treasure of 657 Buddhist manuscripts, and received far more than the amnesty he requested (with careful foresight, in advance) from the emperor for leaving China against imperial orders. He was received as the most celebrated monk in the land and treated with honor until his death, twenty-one years after his return.

In his remaining years following his journey, Hsüan-tsang translated 74 of the texts he brought back. As a pilgrim in search of religious documents, Hsüan-tsang also spread knowledge of China in the west, and brought information back to eastern Asia. Because the T'ang emperor was more interested in "the rulers, the climate, the products, and the customs in the land of India to the west of the Snowy Peaks" than he was in esoteric Indian scripture, Hsüan-tsang wrote *The Great T'ang Record of the Western Territories*. For centuries this was China's principal handbook on the lands beyond its western borders.

Hsüan-tsang is perhaps most significant for the role he played in a larger process—the spread of Buddhist ideology. China's "golden age of Buddhism," from before Hsüan-tsang's time until the eighth century, was also the time that Buddhism spread to its greatest extent ever, from the western edge of the Middle East throughout the rest of Asia, including Japan and Indonesia. This fleeting era of religious unity, however, transformed Asia in ways that can still be felt.

Works Cited and Suggestions for Further Reading

Chen, Kenneth
1974   *Buddhism in China: A Historical Survey*. Princeton: Princeton University Press.

Helms, Mary
1988   *Ulysses' Sail: An Ethnographic Odyssey of Power, Knowledge, and Geographical Distance*. Princeton: Princeton University Press.

Waley, Arthur
1952   *The Real Tripitaka*. London: George Allen & Unwin.

Yu, Anthony C.
1977   *Journey to the West*. Chicago: University of Chicago Press.

Vikings and Eskimos

T he Vikings, the Scandinavian mariners who plundered European coasts from the eighth through the tenth centuries, are
not remembered for their gentle manners. The *Groenlendinga
Saga,* one of the Norse heroic narratives, begins by telling how, because of some killings, Thorvald and his son Erik the Red left Norway
for Iceland. By this time, AD 982, Iceland was extensively settled. Erik
married Thjodhild, and they had a son, who bore the name Leif
Eriksson. After more killings, expulsion from one town, and fights
with other men at another, Erik was banned from Iceland.

> He fitted out his ship for sea in Eiriksvag, and told the people there that
> he meant to look for the land that Gunnbjörn UlfKrakuson had sighted
> when he was stormdriven west across the ocean—Gunnbjarnarsker, or
> Gunnbjörn's Skerries. He would be coming back, Erik said, to get in
> touch with his friends should he discover that land. (Jones 1986)

In AD 984, Erik the Red found the land Gunnbjörn had described
and set out to build a new colony: "He called the country he had discovered Greenland, for he argued that men would be drawn to go
there if the land had an attractive name."

Sixteen years later, a prosperous and widely traveled Norse captain
named Bjarni Herjolfsson sailed from Europe to Iceland, where he
was in the habit of spending every other winter with his father. On
his arrival that winter, however, Herjolfsson found that his father
had sold his farm and gone to Erik's colony on Greenland, and so he
followed in his fifty-foot sailing ship. He had no map of the route or
compass (nor did anyone else at that time), and he was going to a

143

place he had never been. He ran into bad weather and was swept to a coast that did not answer to the formidable descriptions of the mountains and glaciers of Greenland.

Bjarni Herjolfsson had found the coast of Labrador, the easternmost part of continental North America, a land covered with forests and low hills. But he was looking for his father, not a New World, so he turned around without landing and sailed two days back to Greenland. This makes Bjarni Herjolfsson the first European on record ever to have seen the New World, and about the most forgotten name in the history of the "discovery" of the Americas (among those whose names we do know). The 500th anniversary of Herjolfsson's voyage would have fallen only eight years after Columbus landed in the Caribbean. But neither Columbus—who traveled to Iceland on one of his early voyages as a merchant seaman—nor anyone else among the fifteenth-century scholars and sailors interested in sailing west across the Atlantic was aware of Herjolfsson or his discovery.

Herjolfsson told the story of his detour to Erik and others, and later Leif Eriksson went to explore this new coast. Not to be outdone by his father's euphemistic labeling of Greenland, Leif called the place *Vínland hit góda*, or "Wineland the good," although wine grapes could not possibly grow there. (Some argue that this wild exaggeration results from a mistaken transmission of the Norse sagas, whereby *vin*, or "grassland," was confused with *vín*, "wine.")

On Vinland, the Vikings discovered people, whom they called Skraelings (barbarians). Just who these people were has been a subject of scholarly debate. They may have been arctic sea people—Eskimos or their predecessors—but the archeologist Robert McGhee proposes that they were Algonquian-speaking Indians of the Atlantic northeast, who could have traveled this far north each summer. Whoever these Skraelings were, the first recorded interaction between New World and Old World people was a disaster—and almost eerily prophetic for subsequent European-Indian interactions. Leif lent his ship to his brother Thorvald, who sailed for the North American coast. Thorvald found a large, flat headland on a forested bay, walked around for a while, and declared, "This is a lovely place, and here I should like to make my home."

> Then they made for the ship, and saw three mounds on the sands up inside the headland. They walked up to them and could see three skin-

boats there, and three men under each. So they divided forces and laid
hands on them all, except for one who got away with his canoe. The
other eight they killed, and afterwards walked back to the headland,
where they had a good look around and could see various mounds on
up the fjord which they judged to be human habitations.

Act 1, Scene 2 of the encounter of two worlds begins an hour or
two later, after Thorvald and his men have had a nap:

"Rouse ye, Thorvald, and all your company, if you would stay alive.
Back to your ship with all your men, and leave this land as fast as you
can!" With that there came from inside the fjord a countless fleet of
skin-boats and attacked them.

Although Thorvald was killed in this battle, he turns up in later
stories, one indication that the sagas are far from reliable historical
documents. They were often written down centuries after the events
they describe took place. But the archeological site of L'Anse aux
Meadows, on the northern tip of the island of Newfoundland, testi-
fies unequivocally to the Norse presence there.

The attempts to colonize Vinland lasted a few more years after
Thorvald's misadventure but ultimately were unsuccessful. According
to the sagas, the venture was doomed by Skraeling hostility and internal fighting among the Norse. Possibly Vinland was also just too
far away from Greenland, Iceland, and the Norwegian homeland for
a colony to survive there. Greenland ultimately suffered the same
fate, but more slowly.

According to the testimony of the Norse sagas, Erik the Red did not
find people on the southern tip of Greenland, only "habitations of
men, fragments of boats of skin, and stone artifacts, from which it
may be seen that the same kind of people had passed that way as
those that inhabited Vinland, whom the Greenlanders called Skraelings." Apart from this observation, there is very little mention of interactions with New World people on Greenland in the early years.
The *Historia Norvegiae* (a history by an unknown author written
about AD 1170) records fights with the Skraelings about AD 1150, and
there are early descriptions of them as "horribly ugly, hairy, and
swarthy, with great black eyes." For the most part, however, until the
final days of the Norse colonization of Greenland, in the 1400s, the
island's cohabitants are scarcely mentioned.

The Skraelings whom the Vikings first encountered on Greenland, or at least those who shared the island with the Norse for most of the time that followed, were the Eskimos. Historians and archeologists concerned with this era call them the Thule; their modern-day descendants are more properly known as the Inuit. By coincidence, both the Thule and the Norse had reached Greenland at about the same time, setting to work to colonize the island as a new extension of their territory. Neither were Greenland's first settlers, however: People had already lived there for nearly 3,000 years.

The first colonizers of Greenland did not head for the relatively mild southern tip chosen by the Norse, but instead colonized the northern tip, the most northerly bit of land in the world. Lying just 450 miles from the pole, the land is now called Peary Land, after the admiral. When they arrived, these first inhabitants were already well adapted to life above the Arctic Circle, making tools that archeologists assign to the arctic small tool tradition. They lived in small tents (less than ten feet in diameter) during both winter and summer and moved their settlements often. Unlike the later Thule, however, they preferred to hunt land mammals such as musk ox and caribou instead of sea mammals, and the archeological evidence that they used dogsleds and kayaks is equivocal.

In Greenland and the eastern part of arctic North America, these early inhabitants slowly transformed their lifestyle and material repertoire into what archeologists call the Dorset tradition. These "Paleo-Eskimos" hunted both land and sea mammals, occupying some settlements for longer and longer periods. Dorset artifacts are more like those that Thule and later Inuit of the northern ice might have used—dogsleds; shoes for snow and ice; kayak parts; large knives similar to those used more recently to make snow houses, or igloos; and harpoons for hunting seals, walruses, and even larger arctic sea mammals.

The earliest Vikings to reach Greenland may have encountered people of the Dorset tradition, but the latter may have already been replaced by the Thule, who were moving from west to east. The origins of the Thule people are obscure, but the similarity of their culture to that found in the western Arctic suggests that they traveled from Siberia, the Bering Strait, and northern Alaska across 5,000 miles of frozen coasts, pack ice, glacial outlets, seasonal passages of open water, and hundreds of islands of the Canadian Arctic. Their superior adaptation to the arctic environment allowed them to cross this territory in a few centuries or less, displacing or assimilating the local groups they encountered. The Thule were emphatically sea people, hunting seals, walruses, and especially baleen whales (their favorite was the bowhead whale, which averages forty feet in length and weighs about forty tons).

There is good archeological evidence for Thule settlements on the coast of Greenland by AD 1100 and some suggestion that the first Thule migrants arrived even earlier. Don Dumond's interesting and readable book *The Eskimos and Aleuts* (1987) puts Thule people on Ruin Island off the coast of northern Greenland before AD 1000. And Moreau Maxwell, in *Prehistory of the Eastern Arctic* (1985), discusses the carbon–14 dating of the early Thule expansion and suggests that the dates for the first wave of immigrants might be in the 900s, rather than the 1000–1100 date usually assumed (although he also warns that radiocarbon dating in the Arctic is a very tricky business). According to Maxwell, one of the surprising points

> is the evidence emerging since the 1970s of strong Norse contact. Since the Norse sagas refer to voyages no farther north than Upernivik (73° north latitude) and then only in the fourteenth century, it had long been assumed that Thule sites with metal objects must have been late in the sequence. It is now clear that the Norse were penetrating northwards at least as far as 79° north latitude less than 50 years after the initial Norse settlement of Brattalid [Erik's farm] on southern Greenland.

Other recent archeological research shows Thule settlers moving steadily down the coasts from northern Greenland, trading walrus ivory for European goods.

The Norse colony in Greenland consisted of two scattered settlements, Brattalid and other homesteads to the east and another group sixty miles to the west. What became of them? The question has been debated since the colony failed. The archeologist Thomas McGovern examines the question from many angles in a fascinating article, "Cows, Harp Seals, and Church Bells: Adaptation and Extinction in Norse Greenland" (1980). He looks at fluctuating global climate, the Norse economy, the hierarchical organization of the colonists' society, and their interactions with the Thule. The question that underlies his discussion is, why did the Norse hold so strongly to unsuccessful European ways, when the Thule offered an ever-present example of better ways of surviving in Greenland?

McGovern concludes that several factors are involved. For one thing, the Norse economy worked all right when the climate was good but was unstable when it deteriorated after 1200, during the period of global cooling known as the Little Ice Age. Ultimately he blames the demise of the colony on the Greenlander elite, who held the outpost to old and ineffective ways until it could no longer survive.

A report from about 1340 comments that "now the Skraelings have the entire West Settlement; but there are horses, goats, cows and sheep, all wild. There are no people, neither Christians nor heathens." Did the Skraelings kill all the colonists? It is doubtful, for even though their relations were sometimes violent, they had lived side by side for a long time, the Thule near the mouths of the fjords and the Norse deeper within. More likely, the colony grew smaller and smaller and less able to sustain itself, while events in northern Europe made Scandinavian traders less willing to cross the dangerous Atlantic to trade with those who remained. The colony is last mentioned in documents from 1409, and the archeological evidence suggests that the eastern settlement was completely deserted by the end of the 1400s.

The descendants of the Thule, the Inuit, eventually occupied all of Greenland's coast. They took Admiral Peary to the North Pole and still live on the island.

Works Cited and Suggestions for Further Reading

Boorstin, Daniel J.
1983   *The Discoverers*. New York: Random House.

Dumond, Don
1987   *The Eskimos and Aleuts*. London: Thames & Hudson.

Jones, Gwen
1986   *The Norse Atlantic Saga*. Oxford, UK: Oxford University Press.

Maxwell, Moreau
1985   *Prehistory of the Eastern Arctic*. New York: Academic Press.

McGovern, Thomas
1980   Cows, Harp Seals, and Church Bells: Adaptation and Extinction in
         Norse Greenland. *Human Ecology*, v8, p245–275.

Morison, Samuel Eliot
1971   *The European Discovery of America: The Northern Voyages*. New York:
         Oxford University Press.

Disney
Dissonance

A few years ago I spent the summer with my wife and four-year-old daughter in the small town of Cholet, in the Loire Valley of western France. In the surrounding countryside, we visited some of the magnificent chateaux built between the twelfth and eighteenth centuries by some of Europe's most powerful families. Passing these off to a four-year-old as "castles," however, presented a problem, for none of the buildings measured up to what she thought of as *real* castles. They were nothing like Walt Disney's castles—places associated with stories of princesses and evil stepmothers and dragons—which have soaring spires, flying pennants, ramparts, moats, drawbridges, thrones, and dungeons.

What we saw were very nice houses with thick rock walls, some with moats and well-planted gardens. We explained that these were real castles, where the more down-to-earth versions of the stories happened. But to a four-year-old—who with great forbearance tolerated a land where all the other kids babbled incomprehensibly while her parents ate well and drank wonderful glasses of Vouvray, Sançerre, and Muscadet de Sèvre et Maine—this talk of castles was clearly a case of bait and switch.

All of which led us to visit Eurodisney, east of Paris. I was somewhat reluctant to go, if for no other reason than the considerable entrance fee ($120 for three). But then again, I was curious to see what was behind all the commotion in the French and American press. After opening with great fanfare in April 1992, Eurodisney was reportedly suffering from financial problems. In part, this was attributed to a strong negative reaction by many of the French toward what they perceived as American cultural imperialism. (As it happens, we found that in August all the big hotels near the park were booked solid and the place was mobbed, suggesting that the rumors of Eurodisney's demise were exaggerated.)

Driving from Paris, we passed through a plain reminiscent of central Kansas—a basically flat landscape with rolling hills and agricultural fields. Then, with the spires of the Eurodisney castle looming in the distance like the Emerald City of Oz, we came to the fringes of the park, marked by the first of tens of thousands of newly planted trees. The road wound through a series of landforms that seemed characteristically Disneyesque—heavily planted earthen ridges rose just above eye level on both sides. These disorienting features control the way dramatic views unfold in the created landscape and hide the infrastructure of the huge theme park, with its delivery vans and garbage trucks. We parked half a mile from the gate in the Goofy section of the sprawling parking lots and rode conveyer belts to the entrance, inundated with theme songs.

Eurodisney is in many ways spectacular and breathtaking, presenting perfected, idealized worlds with imaginative twists and turns. Every tile, stone, and trash can is custom-made. The "imagineers" are responsible for this; they are a large group of designers who craft wood, metal, plastic, plaster, and concrete to fit their extraordinary vision. In Discoveryland an ornate Victorian blimp docks in a ten-story-high ultramodern structure; nearby, a blasted spacescape of eroded metal and crystalline stone overflows with fountains of sparkling water. And in the center of the park is Sleeping Beauty's Castle—a *real* castle, with proper pennants and ramparts and a rather terrifying robotic dragon in its dungeon.

Even the rocks are manufactured. Someday I would like to research and write the comprehensive geology of Disney. Everywhere I looked, the walls and structures were covered in what one would certainly take for stone. It is all, however, something else—something that without my rock hammer I could not positively identify as plastic, fiberglass, or plaster. I counted twenty-four kinds of "rock," and within them all kinds of variations—granite slabs, slate tiles, blocks of dolomite, flaking shales, sparkling micaceous composites, lots of golden limestone, and others that resembled nothing I know of in the real world. There was, I might add, plenty of time to observe these materials as we inched our way along looping lines, waiting to get on the rides.

We spent half a day in lines, on rides, and touring the attractions, and at noon encountered one of Eurodisney's cultural and logistical problems. When midday arrives, the French expect to sit down to a proper meal, complete with table, waiter, wine and bread, and the other basic amenities one would find in any small French town. These things are difficult to find at Eurodisney, and expensive if you do find them. For Americans this is less of a problem; they eat on an irregular schedule and with different expectations.

Despite the pronounced American theme of Mainstreet, U.S.A., the easiest fast food to find at Eurodisney is the French version—crusty baguettes split and filled with butter, cheese, and ham. After buying these, one must then find a seat where one can, which in our case was on the curb. On our second day we found a better way around the lunch problem by asking the French "cast members" where to eat. They directed us to Walt's, a quiet restaurant with good food; wonderful service; and in the background, classical string quartet arrangements of the theme songs we had been swimming through. And they served good French wine, even though we had been told wine was forbidden in Eurodisney.

Most extraordinary at Walt's was the decor. The room we were in combined Victorian and Art Nouveau styles with an unusual futuristic twist. The dining room chairs were carved with the dials and trappings of time machines, and everywhere the mahogany woodwork was sculpted in flowing forms. The effect was reminiscent of the interior of Captain Nemo's submarine in the film *20,000 Leagues Under the Sea*. Original sketches and models for that film were all around, along with a remarkable collection of documents and illustrations from other projects. The restaurant and the surrounding art exemplified Walt Disney's utopia—nineteenth-century sensitivities and social order coupled with twenty-first–century technology.

The utopia reflected in the sketches on the walls of Walt's is perhaps Disney's best, unassailable because it is an idealized world that does not yet exist. The fantasies dealing with the past run into trouble, however, because no matter how mythical and ahistorical their presentation (as in the Peter Pan–inspired pirates section or Frontierland's Old West), there is a historical past haunting the background. I was especially aware of this at Buffalo Bill's Wild West Show, where you can "conquer the West from your dinner table." The conquering theme was never spelled out, but the way the show was staged made it clear that the only thing that needed conquering was the stereo-typical Indians.

Nearly all the attractions in the park are linked to the stories told in Disney films. Although many of these stories are based on European works or folktales, they often differ from the more faithful versions that Europeans learn as children. In Sleeping Beauty's Castle, the cen-terpiece of Eurodisney, we climbed the stairs of the grand hall and walked through scenes from Disney's story of Sleeping Beauty. As we milled about in the crowd, we saw parents from all over Europe mak-ing quick interpretations—apparently trying to connect the Disney characters and events to those that their children knew.

Disney's *Sleeping Beauty* is but the prologue to a more sinister tradi-tional tale, recounted in complete form by the French writer Charles Perrault (1628–1703). Perrault's version begins much the same as Dis-ney's: A king and queen have a daughter after great difficulty con-ceiving. They invite the kingdom's seven fairies to the christening, so that each might bless the child with a gift. But they neglect to invite an old fairy who has been in seclusion for fifty years. The daughter is given gifts by six of the fairies—beauty, wit, grace, and so on—but the old fairy puts a spell on her that will cause her to die from pricking her finger on the spindle of a spinning wheel. The last good fairy, who has hidden in the draperies suspecting some meanness from the old one, comes out and commutes the spell to a sleep of 100 years.

The princess grows up and, as foretold, pricks her finger and falls into her deep sleep. The seventh good fairy puts all the servants in the castle to sleep as well, so that the princess will not awaken alone, and causes thick vines to grow up around the castle. After a century, another family is on the throne (thus is incest averted), and the story of the princess and the spell has been nearly forgotten. The king-dom's prince is intrigued by the castle and enters, finding the princess. With his kiss, he breaks the spell. At this point, in Disney's version, the couple then live happily ever after.

Perrault's story continues, however. The prince and princess marry and have two children, but the prince keeps all this secret from his parents, the king and queen. Although the prince loves the queen, he

does not trust her, for she is of the race of ogres. He fears she will suc-
cumb to her ogreish impulses, which include a taste for human flesh,
especially that of tender young children.

The old king dies and the prince takes the throne, acknowledging
his marriage to Sleeping Beauty and bringing her and their children
into the capital. Soon he goes to war, however, and has to leave the
kingdom and his family in the care of the old queen. The ogre in the
queen soon expresses itself, and she orders the cook to serve up first
the children and finally Sleeping Beauty herself for dinner. The clever
cook fools her by substituting other meats and hiding the intended
victims.

But the queen discovers the ruse and commands them all, including the cook and his family, to be bound and thrown into a tub
crawling to the brim with toads and poisonous snakes. The prince,
now king, returns in the nick of time to save them, and his enraged
mother throws herself headfirst into the tub and is devoured. Only
then, in Perrault's version, do they all live happily ever after.

The characters in Perrault's story are enmeshed in the politics of
families and kingdoms and have difficult decisions to make. Good
and evil are not spelled out so clearly as in Disney's tale; the villain-
ous characters' evil is an inescapable part of their nature, which includes both good and evil, and is not the result of their jealousy or
ambition. Perrault's *Sleeping Beauty* is a more complex fable, which
may be read at several levels and with several morals. Like the Disney
version of *Sleeping Beauty*, the other Disney films adapted from European sources—*Cinderella, Snow White, The Little Mermaid, Pinocchio,
Sword in the Stone, Robin Hood, Alice in Wonderland, Beauty and the
Beast, Peter Pan*—are very much altered. Mickey Mouse, an original
Disney creation, is popular in Europe, but the other characters do not
seem to inspire as strong a reaction. The films have at their foundations a set of values that Disney believed in—for example, that
through the unwavering conviction of moral individuals, good will
prevail over evil, even against seemingly impossible odds. These values struck such a chord among Americans that the movies became
very successful. But one cannot expect audiences from other cultures
to react to Disney's message in the same way.

After our second long, hot day of lines and crowds and last dashes
here and there, we left Disney's world and headed for western France,
encountering Paris's all too real rush-hour traffic. The next day, still

heading west, we stopped at another chateau (we had stopped calling them castles) and experienced firsthand what it is like to see a theme-park representation of a story different from the version we heard as children.

We took our daughter to the Chateau d'Usse, said to have been the setting Charles Perrault had in mind while writing his version of *Sleeping Beauty*. In rooms high in the chateau, a series of scenes from the story were created with props and mannequins. Some of the scenes worked equally well for both the Perrault version and Disney's, but where they applied only to the older plot, we had a lot of explaining to do.

Child: Where's Maleficent?

Parent (pointing to a mannequin that looked as if it were modeling royal bathrobes): That's Maleficent.

Child: No, where's the evil fairy, the mean one?

Parent: That's her.

(Child gives a sideways glance meaning, "Is this a joke?")

Thereafter we stayed away from European attractions that portrayed versions of stories that were different from those our daughter knew. I think that some Europeans have decided to steer clear of Eurodisney for similar reasons.

Works Cited and Suggestions for Further Reading

Perrault, Charles
1984   *Belle au bois dormant* (The Sleeping Beauty). Illustrated by John Collier. Mankato, MN: Creative Education.

Walt Disney Staff
1997   *Disney's Sleeping Beauty: Classic Storybook*. Mouse Works.

Caribbean Connections

I began carrying out work in the Caribbean because I was interested in the way the Taíno people of the Greater Antilles developed complex political systems between AD 800 and 1500. When I first went to the islands I knew little of Caribbean culture and history. My academic interests ended about 1525 or so.

Since my first visit, my research interests have become broader and the experience of living and working in the modern Caribbean is no doubt part of the reason. Although still interested in Caribbean prehistory, I have also become interested in cultural contact and change in the Caribbean, and in the political uses of the past. The complex history of the region, parts of which come through in the chapters in this section, includes the interactions of Taíno and Island Caribs, Europeans, Africans, and Asians. Through time the Caribbean has become one of the most culturally diverse areas in the world, with different languages and histories on almost every island (and sometimes two very different cultures sharing one island, as with Haiti and the Dominican Republic, or French and Dutch Saint Martin/Sint Maarten).

In some ways the Caribbean is a microcosm of the processes of culture contact in the Americas. It was the site of the first collision of European and American culture in the aftermath of Columbus's voyages, and it has been a center of cultural interaction and change ever since. This interaction has not resulted in anything like a "melting pot"; if anything it has led to increased cultural diversification. New Caribbean musical styles are constantly being adopted in North American and world musical genres. The creativity of Caribbean artists is in part a product of their rich milieu of culture contact. In situations where cultural forms are in flux or where many groups are competing, little is to be gained by clinging to traditional forms or the status quo. Innovation succeeds in contexts of cultural interaction.

The Caribbean has also been the center of great tragedies, from the near extinction of the indigenous people to the centuries of the most horrific forms of institutional slavery. These aspects of Caribbean history loom large in modern social and political spheres, and are everywhere inescapable. In my experience this history has not had a crippling impact on the people of the Caribbean. In fact, it is perhaps the opposite. On French-, English-, and Spanish-speaking islands in the Caribbean it seems as if there is a greater sense of self-worth and self-confidence than one finds elsewhere in the Americas. Perhaps this comes with surviving such a difficult past.

A final theme that runs through these chapters is that new cultures emerge in situations of culture contact. The search for "Africanisms" and "indigenous contributions" to West Indian culture are important, but cultures have a whole and integral quality that cannot be understood by looking for the sources of all the parts that compose them. As I argue in the first chapter in this section, Jamaican culture is something new that came into being on Jamaica itself. One can see aspects of Jamaican culture that are reminiscent of Africa and Europe, and aspects that resonate with other former British colonies ("Cricket, anyone?"), but at its core, it is uniquely Jamaican. This principle applies to the rest of the Caribbean and the rest of the Americas.

Saint George
and Juncanoo

The village of Gingerland is strung out along a couple of roads on the small Caribbean island of Nevis. The main route around the island passes through the village, another heads down to the sea, and a third turns inland toward the island's 3,000-foot-tall volcanic cone. The dominant buildings are two stone churches; near the village center, a bridge crosses a ravine, filled with breadfruit and papaya trees, and small shops line the road. Some inhabitants of Gingerland's large cemetery lived and died when Nevis was the center of Britain's New World empire and the North American colonies were but the troublesome and unprofitable periphery. A few hundred people, more or less, live in the village, depending on where you draw its boundaries. But at Christmas, people from all over Nevis and the surrounding islands come here to see the masquerade.

The "captain"—an older man well known in the community— leads a dozen or so costumed male dancers through the village. These men wear colorful shirts and trousers, or sometimes skirts, on which small mirrors and bells have been sewn. Trailing ribbons decorated with more flashing mirrors and tinkling bells, they dance to the rhythm of two drums (a deep kettledrum and a deeper bass) and a simple wood or tin fife.

Other groups of dancers wear far more elaborate costumes, with crowns of peacock feathers and striking gowns. Still others are dressed in parodies of European clothes of another era and masks of wire mesh painted a startling pink. Some athletic dancers wear minimal costumes and carry bows and arrows; as they dance wildly, the most adept throw tomahawks into the air and catch them without looking. The devilish protagonist of the island's popular "bull play" may appear, dressed in a red suit and fierce mask with bull's horns attached.

At first the music sounds like a military march, but the fife has an exaggerated and somewhat satirical air. The music shifts, and the dancers glide into a stylized waltz; as the beat accelerates, men and women dance a hot rumba, very close to each other but not touching. At each change the music stops abruptly, freezing the dancers in their steps. Here is the cast of Nevis's historical drama over the past five centuries—people whose ancestors were from Africa, Europe, and the New World itself. The masquerade features them all, and the music and dance tell stories of the ways they interacted.

The celebrations of the holiday season in the Caribbean have an ancient texture to them, but of course they are of the past five centuries' creation. The islands of the Caribbean that Columbus saw in his voyages are radically transformed today. The people, their cultures and languages, even the terrain and plants and animals, are all vastly different. The modern Caribbean is a mosaic of different languages, nationalities, cultures, and histories. Traveling from Jamaica to Haiti to Puerto Rico, and on to Nevis, Guadeloupe, Barbados, or Trinidad, one has the sense of moving through different worlds (or perhaps through strangely similar worlds at different times). Some themes, however, have an almost-tangible presence throughout the region, none as strong as the echoes of the African slave trade.

Because of the holiday season, December is the time of year when stories of the past seem to have special importance. In North America, as elsewhere, to celebrate Christmas, trees are forced through living room doors and loaded down with an anthropologist's dream of symbolic ornaments—birds; donkeys; candles; stars; and sleighs with fat, bearded gentlemen in strange red suits. Mistletoe is hung and rings of ornamented foliage are placed on doors. To celebrate Hanukkah, the candles of the menorah are lighted one by one and the dreidel is spun. All these things demand the recitation of stories that account for them, although sometimes the traditions that give meaning to the customs are nearly lost from everyone's memory. (Who was King Wenceslas, anyway? And what is a dreidel?)

In the Caribbean, traditions are different from island to island, and Gingerland's masquerade is just one of many observances. In 1774,

Edward Long described a Jamaican masquerade featuring an important character called John Canoe:

> In the towns, during Christmas holidays, they have several tall robust fellows dressed up in grotesque habits, and a pair of ox horns on their head, sprouting from the top of a horrid sort of visor, or mask, which about the mouth is rendered very terrific with large boar-tusks. The masquerader, carrying a wooden sword in his hand, is followed with a numerous crowd of drunken women, who refresh him frequently with a cup of aniseed-water, whilst he dances at every door, bellowing out John Connu! with great vehemence.

Who is John Canoe? Edward Long thought he represented John Conny, a celebrated African king involved with the Prussians in the slave trade ("Conny" is a corruption of the German *König*, or "king"). In 1816, however, Matthew Gregory "Monk" Lewis described John Canoe in less fearsome terms, "dressed in a striped doublet, and bearing upon his head a kind of pasteboard house-boat, filled with puppets, representing, some sailors, other soldiers, others again slaves at work on a plantation, &c." Perhaps the dancer and his headpiece represented the slave trade itself, with soldiers and sailors taking Africans into bondage. Some speculate instead that the character of John Canoe was modeled after Noah, who saved humankind from the Old Testament deluge.

It has been suggested that the name John Canoe is a corruption of the French *gens inconnus* ("unknown folks") and refers to the movement of French speakers from Haiti to Jamaica in 1795. Some elements from Haiti did indeed enter the festivities after that time. One such, important to the John Canoe celebrations in the nineteenth and early twentieth centuries, was the parade of "set girls," groups of young women who dressed in elaborate formal gowns, "pin for pin alike, and carried umbrellas or parasols of the same color and size, held over their nice showy, well-put-on toques" (Scott 1833).

There is an older John Canoe, however. In *Jamaica Talk* (1961), the linguist Frederic Cassidy argues that the name is what is important, and that the boat (like many parts of the performance) was added later. In the West African language Ewe, which is spoken today in Nigeria and is related to several west coast languages, *dzhon* means a sorcerer or magician and *kens* means something terrible that can cause death. The combined form, *dzhon ko-nu,* means a powerful and dangerous shaman. In Jamaica and elsewhere in the Caribbean, and in most of the rest of the African American New World, such a person is now generally called an Obeah-man.

John Canoe was one of many West African contributions to Jamaican culture. To cite just one other example, the most popular Jamaican folktales are stories of Anancy, the trickster spider; they deal with the same plots and themes as the stories of West Africa's *anansesem* (spider stories), sometimes mirroring them nearly word for word. The similarities are remarkable, considering that the ancestors of those now living in Africa and the New World parted company in Thomas Jefferson's time or before.

Jamaican stories and performances rework African themes and weave them together with elements of Judeo-Christian, Native American, and even classical traditions. "Monk" Lewis, in his journal for 1815, records a John Canoe celebration in which the figures on parade included Britannia carrying a trident and the coat of arms of Great Britain (portrayed by a horribly embarrassed young woman), the king and queen, Admiral Lord Nelson, and British mummers. The Yoruba god Ogun, patron of smiths and metalworking, may appear in the form of (or sometimes alongside) Saint George, Saint James, or Saint John. Others who have proved popular over the years include Nanny and Cudjoe, revered leaders of Jamaican maroons (blacks who escaped slavery and set up free communities in the mountains), as well as General Jackson, who brutally put down a rebellion in 1865.

So who is John Canoe—an African king in league with Prussians; a biblical Noah; a leader of Haitian "unknown folk"; a West African Obeah-man; or some other, unidentified personality? The only answer that is accurate and faithful to John Canoe's complicated origins is that he is a Jamaican. The Jamaican tradition of John Canoe combines all the contributing sources.

Such fusions are found in all Caribbean holiday pageants. Recent Christmas plays on Nevis have featured, among many others, David and Goliath, Saint George and the dragon, Mussolini and Haile Selassie, Ferdinand and Isabela, Moses and the children of Israel, mummies, and a multifaceted character named the Black Prince of Palestine.

Times change and cultures change with them (or maybe vice versa). Now the Christmas dances themselves are becoming less popular: Gingerland's Christmas fame has declined greatly in the last generation. In *Christmas Sports in St. Kitts-Nevis* (1984), Kittitian-born

Frank Mills writes, "The overwhelming majority of Kittitians and Nevisians under thirty years of age have never heard of half the different kinds of sports mentioned, and have witnessed even fewer. And there are many nationals over fifty who can add perhaps another dozen [to the eight I have described]."

John Canoe too is becoming a forgotten figure. Even in the early 1800s, the John Canoe dance in Jamaica was coming under pressure to change. The Reverend R. Bickell, an abolitionist, wrote in 1825 that "most of those who had become Christians were ashamed to join in it." This adds weight to the interpretation that, at least in part, John Canoe voiced a people's resistance to an inhumane system and signaled their allegiance to an African past at a time of the year when they were able to express themselves most freely. The powerful and disturbing John Canoe became less important at about the time of the abolition of slavery in the British colonies in 1834. Once the centerpiece of the celebration, he became the headliner for an increasingly diverse performance, then a member of the cast, and eventually a character whose story few can remember in any detail.

In 1951, there was an attempt to revive the John Canoe dance with all its characters, and again dissension was voiced. One letter to the editor of Jamaica's *Daily Gleaner* said that "Juncunoo" was obscene, and "many people were taken to court for dancing horse-head, it was so vulgar." We need not lament the passing of this tradition, however. More than likely, the spirit of John Canoe—woven in new ways into the constantly changing West Indian traditions—has been so transformed that despite his presence we no longer recognize him.

Works Cited and Suggestions for Further Reading

Bickell, Reverend R.
1825   *The West Indies as They Are: or, A Real Picture of Slavery*. London: J. Hatchard.

Brathwaite, Edward
1971   *The Development of Creole Society in Jamaica 1770–1820*. Oxford, UK: Clarendon Press.

Cassidy, Frederic G.
1982 [1961]   *Jamaica Talk: Three Hundred Years of the English Language in Jamaica*. London: Macmillan Caribbean (2nd edition).

Letter to the Editor
1951, *Daily Gleaner* (Jamaica), January 2, p2.

Lewis, Matthew Gregory
1969 [1834]   *Journal of a West India Proprietor, Kept During a Residence in
                the Island of Jamaica.* New York: Negro Universities Press.

Long, Edward
1970 [1774]   *The History of Jamaica: or, General Survey of the Ancient and
                Modern State of That Island: With Reflections on Its Situa
                tion, Settlements, Inhabitants, Climate, Products, Commerce,
                Laws, and Government.* New edition with a new introduc
                tion by George Metcalf. London: Frank Cass.

Mills, Frank L., and S. B. Jones-Hendrickson
1984   *Christmas Sports in St. Kitts-Nevis: Our Neglected Cultural Tradition.*
        Basseterre, Saint Kitts–Nevis: F. L. Mills.

Mintz, Sidney W.
1974   *Caribbean Transformations.* Chicago: Aldine.

Scott, Michael
1833   *Tom Cringle's Log.* Edinburgh: W. Blackwood.

Thompson, Vincent Bakpetu
1987   *The Making of the African Diaspora in the Americas 1441–1900.* New
        York: Longman.

Caribbean
Diasporas

A few summers ago I was on Nevis for Culturama, that small West Indian island's celebration of its culture. The capital, Charlestown, overflowed with people, who crowded around makeshift booths on the waterfront to buy drinks and such local delicacies as "goatwater" (a spicy stew of goat meat and breadfruit) and "salt fish" (a stewed concoction made from dried, salted cod—a rather improbable historical holdover of colonial English cuisine in a region where fresh fish is always available). The occasion also featured horse and donkey races, the Culturama Queen competition, a contest for calypso singers from all over the island, and a great deal of music and dancing.

Culturama is an enthusiastic celebration of African American cultural continuity and survival despite centuries of oppression. A few blocks away from the crush of people at the booths, a more tranquil scene commemorates a similar lesson in survival. Surrounded by a stone wall, the Jews' burying ground leaves a gap the size of a couple of house lots in the middle of the bustling town. Although more than 300 years old, it is neatly tended, thanks to the efforts of the Nevisian government and the writer Robert Abrahams, who divides his time between Philadelphia and Nevis.

The twenty or so graves that remain are stone boxes covered by massive stone slabs. Most have a few pebbles and coins on top, put there according to local custom so that the dead will rest in their

165

places and not roam about at night. Placing pebbles on graves is also a Jewish tradition, to show that a grave has been visited recently, but just who adorned these graves is not apparent. Many of the lids are elaborately carved with inscriptions in a combination of Hebrew, English, and Ladino (a language that combines Spanish, Portuguese, and Hebrew elements). Ladino was, and in some parts of the world still is, spoken by the Jews from Spain and Portugal—the Sephardim—who were exiled from the Iberian peninsula in 1492. The dates on the graves range from the 1680s to the mid-1700s, but the Jewish community existed on Nevis before and well after that time span.

The standard view of Nevis's history is that the island was colonized by members of wealthy English families who exploited slave labor for sugar production. The names on these tombstones, however, show this view to be incomplete. Jacob Alvarez, Abraham Isquiao David Gomes, Daniel Cohen, Abraham Bueno de Mez-queto, Solomon Israel, and several members of the Pinheiro family are buried there. (Isaac Pinheiro's tombstone is also there, but, truth to tell, despite his fervent wish to be buried on Nevis, his body actually lies in the Chatham Square cemetery of the congregation of Sherith Israel in New York City.) All were members of a thriving Jewish community that existed throughout the Caribbean at that time.

The most elegant grave in the cemetery is that of Bathsheba Abudiente, who died in childbirth on August 8, 1684. The Hebrew inscription on her tombstone gives her husband's name as Rohiel Abudiente, but a second inscription in English shows that he also went by the name of Rowland Gideon. An old frangipani, or "temple tree," with deep pink flowers leans over the slab. The Hebrew inscription reads:

This heap be witness and the pillar be witness that in its womb rests the modest woman, a woman of valor, crown of her husband, Mrs. Bathsheba, wife of Mr. Rohiel Abudiente, whose spirit was returned to God after she had borne a son buried next to her, on Tuesday, the 28th day of the month of Ab in the year 5444. For she did what was right in the eyes of the Lord. May her soul be bound up in the bond of eternal life.

Many of the other graves in the cemetery have not withstood the years quite so well. In some cases all that remains is a fragment of a tomb lid leaning against another grave, perhaps showing part of a name or a few Hebrew letters.

*The tomb of Bathsheba
Abudiente, who died
August 8, 1684.*

A dirt path still called the Jews' Walk leads south from the cemetery to a nondescript square building full of fifty-five–gallon oil drums, bathtubs, galvanized corrugated roofing, scrap lumber, and other things too useful ever to throw away on a small Caribbean island. The stone facing is of fairly recent construction, but the stonework inside is old and finely worked, with carved columns supporting a vaulted ceiling (the original exterior stones were probably taken for use elsewhere). This building has recently been identified as part of the old synagogue.

Possibly this building adjoined the main chamber of the synagogue, whose location may be marked by the adjacent pile of rubble. It may also have been the building known as the Jews' School, where, along with many others, the young Alexander Hamilton received his earliest education. Born on Nevis in 1755, the future first secretary of the United States Treasury was the son of James Hamilton, a young and recently bankrupt Scot, and Rachael Faucitt Lavien, a woman fleeing an unhappy but undissolved marriage on Saint Croix. Because Rachael was not lawfully free to remarry, their children were considered illegitimate by the Anglican church and refused admittance to the Anglican school. So Alexander learned to read and write and to recite the Decalogue in Hebrew as a pupil of the Jews' School. The Hamilton Museum in Charlestown is undertaking the building's restoration, as funds permit.

Other Caribbean islands have monuments to substantial Jewish communities that existed from the early years of European colonization. The Mikve Israel synagogue on Curaçao, built in 1702, is the oldest synagogue in continuous use in the Americas. According to records from 1715, Jews constituted the majority of Curaçao's white population. On Barbados the synagogue of Kaal Kadosh Nidhe Israel, built in 1654 and for a long time unused, was recently spared from demolition and has been restored. Jamaica was settled by Europeans in the first wave of Spanish colonization after Columbus's voyages, and the island was the home of the earliest Jewish community in the New World. Like many such communities, it was made up of Jews who had been expelled from Spain and Portugal in the late 1400s. Others fled the Iberian peninsula in the sixteenth and seventeenth centuries, as the Spanish Inquisition attempted to identify Jews who had outwardly converted to Christianity but who secretly maintained Jewish traditions. When the English captured Jamaica from Spain in 1655, the Jews joined with the English in exchange for religious tolerance. They were granted British citizenship (something that Jews living in England at the time did not have) and founded a synagogue that very year.

Nevis, although a small island, played more than a minor role in the history of the Caribbean. In the mid-1600s, the survival of the North American colonies was not certain, given the strength of Native American resistance. New York City was Dutch New Amsterdam from its founding in 1624 until 1664. The colonies in the Massachusetts Bay area, especially those founded by religious exiles, were not part of the British government's overall colonial strategy and, in any case, were not very substantial in the seventeenth century. Nor were they as profitable as Nevis and other Caribbean colonies. The Caribbean colonies were the British foothold in the Americas before the Chesapeake Bay colonies became profitable, and they continued as strongholds after the American Revolution.

In the seventeenth and eighteenth centuries, Jews played a large part in the economy of the Caribbean. Wills, journals, and other documents compiled by the American Jewish Historical Society and the Jewish Historical Society of England demonstrate that the Jewish community of Nevis had far-reaching associations with Europe and other European colonies in the New World. Those buried in the cemetery on Nevis, many of whom had lived abroad, had had family and business contacts in Lisbon, London, Amsterdam, Calcutta, Brazil, Curaçao, Barbados, Jamaica, Virginia, New York, and Boston. Often these associations were the business links that made Nevis so profitable.

The Atlantic trade in sugar, tobacco, indigo, food, goods, and people was complex, involving exchanges in a half-dozen shifting currencies between markets throughout Europe, Africa, the Caribbean, and the eastern seaboard of North America. Excluded (at least officially) from Spain and Portugal, and discriminated against in much of the rest of Europe, European Jews of the seventeenth and eighteenth centuries found a haven in the Caribbean, where they became traders, shopkeepers, and planters.

The Caribbean was not free of religious intolerance and persecution, however. Nevisian Jews, like most in the Caribbean, were subject to special taxes and prohibitions, and their relations with other groups on the island were often strained. In 1724, the Episcopal minister Robert Robertson wrote to the bishop in London that on Nevis there were

> about 70 householders with their families, being in all (children included) some 300 whites where of one-fourth are Jews, who have a synagogue here and are very acceptable to the country part of the island, but far from being so in the town, by whom they are charged with taking the bread out of Christian mouths. And this, with the encouragement said to be given to the Transient Traders, above what is given to the Settlers, is by many thought to be the true cause of the strange decay of this place—At present there is not above 3 or 4 Christian Families of note in my Parish. (quoted in Stern 1971)

The Jews of Nevis in the seventeenth and eighteenth centuries also owned slaves of African descent. Many whites of even modest means did at that time both in the Caribbean colonies and in North America.

Wills in Nevis contain bequests of slaves, and a 1707 census lists five Jewish heads of households who all together owned forty-three slaves.

About Bathsheba Abudiente, the woman with the elegant gravestone, little is known except that she died in childbirth, preceding her husband in death by thirty-eight years. Much more is known about her husband, Rohiel Abudiente, or Rowland Gideon. His maternal grandfather was Paul de Pina, of Lisbon, whose family lived outwardly as converts to Christianity. Paul traveled from Lisbon to Rome in 1599, supposedly to become a Christian monk, but instead he became more openly Jewish. He went to Brazil, where there was more religious tolerance than in Portugal, and then to Amsterdam, the city where European Jews enjoyed the greatest acceptance. In Amsterdam, Paul joined the synagogue under his Jewish name, Reuel Jessuram. He was married and had a daughter, Sarah Jessuram. Sarah in time married Moses Abudiente, a member of another of Lisbon's respected Jewish families. Their son, Rehiel (Rohiel) Abudiente, was born about 1650.

Rohiel's early life is not well documented, but by piecing together scraps of official records, we may surmise that he had connections and relatives in several parts of the New World. In 1674, he was listed under his anglicized name, Rowland Gideon, as "Ye Jew" on Boston's first tax roster. Subsequently he moved to Barbados, possibly because Jews there were more readily granted the status of permanent resident in the British empire. In 1679, Rowland Gideon received such a letter of "denization," which allowed him to reside in any English colony. That year he moved to Nevis and probably married Bathsheba soon after. He stayed there at least until Bathsheba's death in 1684.

Sometime thereafter he moved to London, where in 1694 he married Esther do Porto, a woman of Portuguese ancestry and a member of a powerful Jewish family in London. In 1699, they had a son they named Sampson (or Samson). In 1701, Rowland Gideon was listed as the reader of the Torah in the Bevis Marks synagogue in London, and the next year he became its treasurer. He appears in official documents a few years later representing the Nevis planters in claims for compensation for the French sacking of Nevis in 1709. These proceedings show that Rowland Gideon still held property on Nevis. In 1722, he died and was buried in London's old Jewish cemetery, Bet Hayim.

Rowland Gideon left a considerable fortune to his son, Sampson, who became one of the most powerful money brokers in the British empire. In 1745, during a period of economic chaos, Sampson arranged a loan of £1,700,000 to the British Crown, and in 1749 he organized a consolidation of the national debt, which reduced its rate of interest. With his close contacts in government, he worked successfully, albeit at great personal cost and against vengeful opposition, to help pass the Jews' Naturalization Act of 1753, which abolished the special taxes and penalties on British Jews.

Sampson Gideon married Jane Ermell, who was from an aristocratic Christian family, and their children were raised in her faith. Sampson withdrew from the synagogue but continued to pay his dues anonymously until his death in 1762. In his will he left £1,000 to the Spanish and Portuguese Jewish community in London, on the condition that he be buried as a Jew in the Jews' cemetery; at the end of his will he commended his soul "to the gracious and merciful God of Israel." He was buried near his father, Rowland Gideon, in Bet Hayim. As for the Jewish community on Nevis, its numbers began to diminish in the late eighteenth century as Nevis's economic fortunes declined. Some members moved back to Europe, and more moved to the newly formed United States. None of the original Sephardic families lives on the island today. But in the twentieth century, another migration of European Jews came to the Caribbean. Just as the expulsion of Jews from Portugal and Spain in 1492 forced the emigration of Sephardic Jews in the sixteenth century, the rise of fascism forced Ashkenazic Jews to flee from many parts of Europe in the years preceding World War II. Jewish immigration to the United States was severely restricted in the 1920s and 1930s, so many made their way to the Caribbean islands, where visas could be obtained. They settled in Jamaica, Barbados, Curaçao, the Dominican Republic, and elsewhere in the region. And there, in what must have seemed like exile, they found Jewish communities, synagogues, and cemeteries that had existed for more than three centuries.

Works Cited and Suggestions for Further Reading

Abrahams, Roger D.
1983   *The Man-of-Words in the West Indies: Performance and the Emergence of Creole Culture*. Baltimore: Johns Hopkins University Press.

Bethencourt, Cardozo de
1925   Notes on the Spanish and Portuguese Jews in the United States, Guiana, and the Dutch and British West Indies During the Seven-

teenth and Eighteenth Centuries. *Publications of the American Jewish Historical Society,* n29, p7.

Bobbé, Dorothy
1955   The Boyhood of Alexander Hamilton. *American Heritage,* June 1955, p4–9, 69–99.

Friedman, Lee M.
1942   *Jewish Pioneers and Patriots.* Philadelphia: Jewish Publication Society of America.

Frommer, Myrna, and Harvey Frommer
1991   Sanctuaries in the Sand. *Caribbean Travel and Life,* September–October 1991, p64–105.

Hershkowitz, Leo
1967   *Wills of Early New York Jews (1704–1799).* New York: American Jewish Historical Society.

Karp, Abraham J. (ed.)
1969   *The Jewish Experience in America; Selected Studies from the Publications of the American Jewish Historical Society.* Five volumes. Edited with introductions by Abraham J. Karp. Waltham, MA: American Jewish Historical Society.

Levine, Robert M.
1993   *Tropical Diaspora: The Jewish Experience in Cuba.* Gainesville: University Press of Florida.

Stern, Malcolm H.
1958   Some Notes on the Jews of Nevis. *American Jewish Archives,* October 1958, p151–159.

Stern, Malcolm H.
1971   The Nevis Story. *American Jewish Historical Quarterly,* v61, n1, p18–32.

Cricket
and Colonialism

June 24, 1950, was a glorious day at Lord's Cricket Ground, which with Ascot and Wimbledon makes up the heart of London society's sporting scene. The royal standard flew from the mast above the pavilion, signaling that King George VI was in attendance. The West Indies team was meeting England for the second in a series of four cricket matches. These were Test matches, that is, first-class (top-level professional) games between national teams. Actually, the West Indies side was multinational.

The Test Series of 1950 came at a critical time in Great Britain's associations with its colonies. In the years following World War II, India, Pakistan, Ceylon (Sri Lanka), Jordan, and Israel had become independent. Leaning more and more toward independence were the many British colonies in and around the Caribbean, including British Guiana (Guyana) on the South American mainland, British Honduras (Belize) in Central America, and more than a dozen major islands. A half century earlier, before the two world wars, the British Empire had embraced a quarter of the earth's population and 12 million square miles, an area about the size of the United States, China, and the former Soviet Union combined. By 1950, the trends against colonialism and toward self-government, coupled with the emergence of a new global economy and balance of power, had reduced the empire to a third of its former size.

173

The West Indies had played Test Series in England before, in the summers of 1928, 1933, and 1939, but the team had never won a single match. And two weeks before, at the Old Trafford cricket oval in Manchester, its initial meeting in this series had gone badly. During its first innings (the first of two times at bat) England scored 312 runs, and the West Indies side was only able to answer with 215. By the end of the match—which took only three days, plus an hour on the morning of the fourth, short by International Test Cricket standards—England had scored a total of 600 runs, beating the West Indies by 202. (For a brief explanation of how runs are scored in cricket, see the appendix to this chapter, "It's How You Play the Game.")

To those who do not know cricket, the scores may seem astronomically high and the pace glacially slow and mind numbing. Each match takes up to five days, with play lasting about six hours each day, and the sides in Test Series play four or five such matches. The deliberate pace is part of cricket's charm for its devotees. International series between favorite rivals come infrequently, so they are a delicacy that can be savored over a whole summer. The cricket fan can make occasional visits to the television to see how things are proceeding or leave the radio on softly all day, letting the BBC announcers, in their endless rambling dialogue, communicate with some subliminal part of the brain. The long matches can be exquisite torture as well, for sometimes one team is so badly behind by the end of the first day that it is very unlikely to recover, but the match must be played out over the next few days to be sure. Jobs are lost in the summers of Test Series; marriages wrecked.

Despite the first defeat, there had been a glimmer of hope for the West Indies' fans in the first Test match. Two young bowlers, just twenty years old and unknown in the cricketing world, had made a strong showing. Jamaica's Alfred Valentine had virtually no experience in first-class cricket, but he dispensed with England's first eight batsmen, allowing only 104 runs. It looked as though he might take all ten wickets, that is, put out all ten batters in the first innings, but his partner Sonny Ramadhin of Trinidad took the final two. Ramadhin was the first West Indian of South Asian ancestry selected for a West Indian side.

Ramadhin and Valentine were "spin" bowlers. All bowlers hurl the ball with a straight arm down the long cricket pitch, trying to hit the wicket on one bounce. The heavily padded batsman stands to one side in front of the wicket and attempts to protect it by hitting the oncoming ball with the bat. Fast bowlers (the kind the West Indies have since become famous for) come tearing up to the pitch with a long run-up, leap high in the air, and fire the ball at speeds in excess of ninety miles per hour. Spin bowlers take a shorter, more leisurely run-up and throw the ball more slowly, about fifty miles per hour. But they put tremendous spin on the ball, so it bounces off at odd angles. There are leg-spinners and offspinners, orthodox and unorthodox spinners, and they bowl flippers, wrong'uns, googlies, and other balls analogous to baseball's change-ups, sliders, and so forth. Ramadhin and Valentine's combination of spin-bowling styles was to prove exceedingly difficult to bat against.

Saturday, June 24, was the opening day of the second Test. "The Three W's," Clyde Walcott, Everton Weekes, and Frank Worrell—who were the same age and had grown up near one another on Barbados—were the heart of what would emerge as a formidable batting side. Batting first, the West Indies ran up 326 runs in its first innings, a very good start. The team batted all that day and into Monday morning (Sunday being a day of rest).

Ramadhin and Valentine then devastated the English in their first innings, allowing only 151 runs. Valentine was an orthodox left-arm spinner who bowled with technical precision and tremendous accuracy. Ramadhin just baffled the batsmen with a peculiar delivery that made it nearly impossible to see how he released the ball or how it was spinning. Ramadhin took five wickets and Valentine four. Prior Jones took the tenth wicket.

Sonny Ramadhin's bowling was portrayed in the British press as mysterious, indecipherable, exotic. Indeed, the whole West Indian side seemed exotic to British spectators, many of whom had never seen people of color. Although a recent census puts England's West Indian population at about half a million, in 1950 only 10,000 people from the West Indies lived in Britain. South Asians were just as rare. In his memoirs, *Island Cricketers,* Clyde Walcott describes an encounter he had that summer with an older woman: "[She] walked past me, gave me an odd sort of look, stopped and came back. She came slowly and warily up to me then, seeming to pluck up courage, rubbed her fingers along my hand and stared at them. But the colour doesn't come off!"

The tour presented difficulties for the West Indian players, who came from British Guiana, Barbados, Trinidad, and Jamaica. For example, they came to hate the bland fare of meat, potatoes, and cabbage, but could not get their hotels to substitute West Indian dishes such as rice and spiced curries. Still, the greatest source of annoyance for the West Indians was that they were seen, in the press and in the cricket oval, as inferior cricketers. The West Indies had previously beaten English teams, although not in England, and was fielding a strong team in the summer of 1950. The players resented being taken lightly.

Of the colonial or former colonial nations, only Australia was regarded in England as a force to be reckoned with. Australia's victory in the Test Series of 1882, the first time England had been defeated on its home ground by a colonial team, had been a climactic event. The following day the *Sporting Times* printed an obituary:

In Affectionate Remembrance

Of

ENGLISH CRICKET

WHICH DIED AT THE OVAL

On

29th August 1882

Deeply lamented by a large circle of sorrowing

friends and acquaintances

R. I. P.

N.B.—The body will be cremated and the

ashes taken to Australia

Ever after, the Test matches between England and Australia had been seen as "playing for the Ashes." (The rivalry continues to the present day, so much so that Margaret Thatcher commented, "The world's a better place when we beat the Australians at cricket.") But the West Indies side was not yet accorded that respect. With evident irritation, Walcott remembers an English cricket official describing the series as "a good opportunity to try out some of the English youngsters for the tour of Australia in the winter," and saying that the West Indies could at least be counted on to play "entertaining" cricket.

When the West Indies came to bat for its second time, late Monday afternoon, England had to prove that the first innings had been a fluke. But the English bowlers could not mount a rally to equal Ramadhin and Valentine's performance. The West Indian batsmen were on a tear, setting records that still hold—Walcott and Gomez put on 211 runs, a record partnership. Walcott alone accounted for 168, and would have added to it, for he was still not out on Wednesday morning when the West Indies "declared," with only six wickets fallen. By declaring, the team made the strategic decision to bring the English side to bat, allowing sufficient time to complete the innings (otherwise the game might end in a draw).

On Wednesday and Thursday, try as they might, the English players could not catch up to the 751 runs scored by the West Indies, and went down to defeat by 326 runs. When the final English batsman fell to Frank (now Sir Frank) Worrell's bowling, West Indians in England and throughout the Caribbean celebrated. Writing in *The Cricketer,* the famous cricket commentator E. W. Swanton described the jubilant scene: "Some [of the West Indians], armed with impromptu instruments, saluted the great occasion with strange noises and a handful with their leader swayed round the field to give a faint reminder to those who know the West Indian islands of the bands at carnival time."

In his memoirs, Clyde Walcott says, "This was our finest hour, with 'those little pals of mine, Ramadhin and Valentine' the special heroes." He was quoting from a popular calypso by Egbert Moore that spread throughout England and the Caribbean. The first verse went:

> *Cricket, lovely cricket,*
> *At Lord's where I saw it;*
> *Cricket, lovely cricket,*
> *Yardley tried his best*
> *But Goddard won the test.*
> *They gave the crowd plenty fun;*
> *Second Test and West Indies won.*
> Chorus: *With those two little pals of mine*
> *Ramadhin and Valentine.*

That Friday, the lead article in the *London Times* gave the West Indies side its due: "Yesterday was their finest hour. They have handsomely laid an All England XI low at Lord's. . . . To win by 326 at the headquarters of cricket, in spite of the brave English recovery led by Washbrook on Wednesday, puts these West Indians for good among the great ones." The article concluded that "West Indian cricket has come of age."

The obvious comparison was with children reaching adulthood. An older British executive I once met on a plane described the 1950 Test in even more explicit terms: "It's like when your son beats you at squash for the first time, isn't it? You regret it and try harder next time, but there it is; it was bound to happen."

For England, the loss was a reminder that the empire was slipping away. The two events may even have been linked to similar historical forces. The patronizing comparison with a child's coming of age was misplaced, however. To cast colonized people as juvenile made no more sense than to portray post–World War II Britain as senile. The world had changed dramatically, and the British Empire of old simply could not exist in the new order.

The West Indian victory was sweeter for having come at Lord's, which Australian Prime Minister Sir Robert Menzies called the great "cathedral of cricket." Walcott noted that "had it come at Trent Bridge or the Oval, at Old Trafford or Headingly, it would still have been a great moment. But it was at the very heart of the game we love . . . and *that* gave the occasion its greatest thrill."

After Lord's, the four-game series stood even. In the next Test, at Trent Bridge, Nottingham, the West Indies proved that the Test at Lord's had not been a miracle. The team beat England decisively, setting several personal and team records. The final Test match was held at the Oval, Kennington, and was one of those matches in which the outcome was determined in the West Indies' first innings. The team scored 503 runs, and then Ramadhin and Valentine were able to hold the English batsmen to 274 runs. With its victory, the West Indies took its place among the best of the cricketing nations. Since 1950, it has been one of the dominant forces in world cricket.

Although the colonial era left deep scars and resentments in Britain's former colonies, in most cases these countries became independent without great bloodshed. Most became members of the Commonwealth, whose charter gave them equal status with Britain. Perhaps emblematic of this relatively peaceful transition, the former colonies' passion for cricket did not diminish with independence.

This was especially true for members of the International Cricket Council—the West Indies, New Zealand, Australia, Sri Lanka, India, Pakistan, South Africa, and Zimbabwe (the council also included many affiliate and associate members).

In *The Tao of Cricket: On Games of Destiny and the Destiny of Games*, which is more a discussion of colonialism and postcolonialism than of cricket, the Indian intellectual Ashis Nandy comments ironically on his compatriots' complete assimilation of the game: "Cricket is an Indian game accidentally discovered by the English. Like chilli, which was discovered in South America and came to India only in medieval times to become an inescapable part of Indian cuisine, cricket, too, is now foreign to India only according to the historians and Indologists. To most Indians the game now looks more Indian than English."

The West Indians feel the same way. As Clyde Walcott writes, "Indeed, cricket comes naturally to the West Indian and I think it's true to say that it is always in his blood."

It's How You Play the Game

Cricket is played by two sides of eleven players each. The sides take turns batting and fielding, and each side comes in to bat twice. The cricket field is an oval with a long axis of from 100 to 150 yards. In the center of the field is the pitch, a carefully prepared rectangle of closely mowed and rolled grass. Two wickets are located twenty-two yards apart, one at each end of the pitch. (A wicket is three upright sticks, the stumps, with two pieces of wood balanced on top, the bails.)

Two batters from the batting side are on the pitch at the same time, one at each wicket. The bowler from the fielding side releases the ball from behind one wicket toward the other (the direction is periodically altered). The ten other fielders are deployed around the oval. The fielding positions include the wicket keeper, who catches the ball and throws it back to the bowler, a number of "slips" beside the wicket keeper to catch barely deflected balls, and an array of others at positions called gully, point, cover, mid-off, square leg, and so on. (If they stand right up close to the batter their position, because of the risk, is called silly mid-off, silly point, and so on.)

The batter toward whom the ball is thrown must protect the wicket from the bowled ball and also attempt to score runs.

When a batter hits a ball, both batters may run down the pitch, changing places. That scores one run. If the ball is hit far enough for them to do so safely, they change places again, scoring as many runs as they can. If the batters hit the ball to the boundary fence, they score four without having to run, and if a fly ball clears the boundary, they score six.

If the bowler can get the ball past a batter and knock off a bail, the batter is out. Batters are also out if they hit a ball that is caught on the fly or try to run but fail to make it to the other end of the pitch before the fielders get the ball back in and knock the bails off the wicket. If batters deflect the ball with their body or pads instead of the bat and keep it from hitting the wicket, they are out "leg before wicket." When ten batters have been retired, the fielding team comes in to bat.

A match is over when both sides have completed their innings or when the time limit is reached. If the side that is behind has not finished its last innings by the end of the final day's play, the match is a draw. To prevent a draw, the winning side can attempt to speed things along by "declaring"—ending its innings before all the batters have batted—or by skipping its second innings altogether.

Works Cited and Suggestions for Further Reading

Cricinfo (web site)
http://www.cricket.org/

James, C. L. R.
1963   *Beyond a Boundary*. New York: Pantheon Books.

Manley, Michael
1988   *A History of West Indies Cricket*. London: Deutsch.

Nandy, Ashis
1989   *The Tao of Cricket: On Games of Destiny and the Destiny of Games*.
            London: Viking.

Ross, Gordon
1976   *A History of West Indies Cricket*. London: Arthur Barker.

Swanton, E. W.
1983   *As I Said at the Time: A Lifetime of Cricket*. London: Willow Books.

Walcott, Clyde
1958   *Island Cricketers*. London: Hodder & Stoughton.

Williams, Marcus (ed.)
1985   *Double Century: 200 Years of Cricket in* The Times. London: Willow
            Books.

The

Cultural

Richness

of the

World

he first two chapters in this section deal with issues concerning Native Americans in the United States today. The first deals with the difficult and emotional question of the repatriation and reburial of Native American skeletal remains unearthed over the past century. This is one of the most difficult and intractable problems in Native American–White relations today. It involves battles over the value we place on the past and about who controls history, and thus the themes in this debate have broad implications for all groups in the Americas. In "Reburying Hatchets," I explore the heartening idea that in spite of the intricate legal battles being fought over the issue, it is through calmer and less obvious dialogues, between Native people and curators, that the matter is being resolved. In this case, and perhaps more generally, issues of cultural difference are resolved person to person, not through legislative acts.

The second chapter in this section celebrates the continuity of Native American culture and tradition. Less than 100 years ago, it was an open question whether Native American people would survive into the twenty-first century. The Indian population reached its lowest point in the 1920 census and has rebounded strongly ever since. The 1990 census counted nearly seven times as many Native Americans as in 1920. Despite this numerical success, government policies in midcentury challenged the ability of Native Americans to survive as tribal entities. The policy of "termination" of tribal status in the 1950s jeopardized many reservations and tribal groups. The termination policy was eventually reversed and tribal status was returned.

In "A Texas Powwow," I explore the elusive quality of cultural continuity on the Alabama-Coushatta reservation in east Texas. As was discussed in the last section, cultures re-create themselves constantly, and it is not easy to say precisely what, if anything, passes unchanged from generation to generation. It would be impossible to conclude, however, after visiting the powwow, that an Alabama-Coushatta identity does not exist. Through centuries of dangerous interactions with other groups—the French, Mexico, the Republic of Texas, and the United States—this people has survived.

The final chapter in this volume celebrates the experience of living in a culturally diverse world, but one in which we share a common humanity. "Trickster Treats" deals with trickster tales, a class of folktale that is famous for being so widespread as to be almost universal. Everywhere, and probably for as long as there has been language, people have invented and retold these tales of characters who attack arrogance and pomposity wherever they find it, but often end up catching themselves in the end. In the ubiquity of these stories it is comforting to have solid (and entertaining) evidence that we are a single human family.

Reburying
Hatchets

I was sharing a picnic table at the Salt Lick Barbecue outside of Austin, Texas, with a group of teenagers from the Caddo Indian Tribe of Oklahoma. They had driven down from Oklahoma for the Caddo Conference, a meeting of archaeologists and Caddo who are interested in the prehistory and early history of the tribe. Some of the teenagers had come as members of a dance group, which was to perform later in the evening. Others had been dragged along by parents who were especially interested in the Caddoan past.

We were trying to eat around enormous beef ribs and talk over the din of the 300 or so participants who were crowded into the hall—about 100 of them Caddo. A young woman wearing the standard outfit of jeans, boots, and western shirt came up to the table and greeted the others with "*Hakuna matata*," and got a few "*Hakuna matatas*" back. My anthropological interest was roused: In most respects these kids looked and acted like anyone else from western Oklahoma, yet they greeted each other in what I took for Caddo. The phrase was curiously familiar, however. Later, hearing my five-year-old daughter singing the *Hakuna matata* song from Disney's *The Lion King*, I had occasion to wonder just how often anthropologists, trying their best to find their way across the gap of cultural difference, get things completely wrong.

Later that night we pushed aside the picnic tables and cleared as much of a dance circle as we could. Caddo singers and drummers set up in the middle of the too-narrow room and we had a somewhat cramped powwow. There were traditional Caddo songs and dances, and other songs borrowed from the northern plains and other southeastern woodlands groups. Some of the dances were only for older women and some for people with particular costumes, but many were intertribal dances in which anyone could participate. To go by popular perceptions, Native Americans and archaeologists are adversaries in a heated debate over returning archaeological collections to the tribes. So a crowded hall full of the two groups dancing together would be "intertribal" indeed. But the Caddo Conference and other similar gatherings across the country call attention to the substantial common interests and common ground that Indians and archaeologists share, as well as to their points of disagreement.

The biggest point of controversy between archaeologists and Native Americans concerns the excavation and curation of human skeletal remains. Many Native people view this as an immoral violation of their ancestors' graves. At the Caddo Conference, getting too close to this complex and perilous issue caused a few tense moments. In one instance an older, rather unreconstructed archaeologist was showing slides from a recent excavation on the Red River between Texas and Oklahoma, the Caddo's traditional homeland. They were the typical illustrations of an archaeological lecture—excavation units, projectile points, pottery, charts, chronological diagrams, and so forth. Then, not knowing of the agreement made by conference regulars nearly twenty years earlier to prevent this, he showed a slide of an excavated burial. It showed a skeleton lying on its left side in a dirt hole, knees drawn up with its right arm limp and the bones of the hand over the knees, like a person in bed, unclothed. In the congenial but somewhat cautious social atmosphere of the Caddo Conference, the slide seemed almost pornographic. It reminded us that how the dead are treated hits people at a visceral level; it cannot be dismissed or taken lightly. The subject of the treatment of the dead also very quickly gets tied up with equally formidable issues of cultural difference.

A few slides at the Caddo Conference, on the other hand, got a far more appreciative reception than they might have received from a room full of archaeologists alone. One particularly elegant pottery vessel, with a deep and lustrous red-brown finish incised with intricate spirals, practically got a round of applause. Another speaker, in a nervous rush to get through his paper, was asked to stop and go back to a slide showing a disk of white shell, carved with intricate cutouts of four rattlesnakes. In the dark auditorium, in the company of Caddoan people who were so interested in the lives and history of their ancestors, these beautiful objects seemed to have special and profound qualities.

New ways of looking at the ancient artifacts are also emerging through the work of contemporary Native American artists who are inspired by the objects recovered through excavations. Modern Native American potters, sculptors, and painters, as well as poets, writers, musicians, and others, interact with the motifs and ideas of the ancient artists in new and vital ways. Archaeologists can participate in this process, as was clear when Jerry Redcorn, a Caddo potter, brought many of her modern pots to the conference. They were faithful reproductions of older Caddoan designs, made in traditional ways, but like every potter she brought her own distinctive style to her work. She spent a lot of time talking and comparing notes with the archaeologists on vessel forms, decoration styles, and manufacturing steps.

Yet most of the pottery and shell carvings and other artifacts being shown had come from excavated graves, and therein lies a serious internal conflict for many Caddo. Those at the conference wanted to know about their people's past, and wanted to see and experience things made by their ancestors, but a lot of this knowledge derives from practices they find morally offensive—the excavation of burials. "So you've got a conflict there," says Mary Cecile Carter, chair of the Cultural and Heritage Committee for the Caddo Indian Tribe of Oklahoma. "You have the conflict that these things should never have been uncovered, and at the same time we have a new appreciation, a new pride, in our heritage because we know that our ancestors did these beautiful things."

For me, sitting in the audience at the Caddo Conference and talking with the archaeologists who came to the conference, it was striking to see that the archaeologists felt a rather parallel sort of conflict. Most archaeologists are very sensitive to being characterized as grave robbers and sincerely respect the feelings of Native American groups about disturbing burials. But sometimes they see no other choice. Many excavations are carried out just before the whole area of the archaeological site is to be bulldozed. Moreover, archaeologists' efforts

to know more about ancient Native Americans come from the conviction that to piece together the prehistory of Native Americans en-
riches all of us, Indian and non-Indian, now and in the future, and
this arguably is a sign of great respect. Information that came from
archaeological research was what debunked the old myths that Native people were "uncivilized." But on the other hand it has been argued that disturbing Native American graves is just another chapter
in the continuing conquest of the Native Americans; participating in
this would be contrary to everything most archaeologists believe. As
Mrs. Carter put it, "You've got a conflict there."

Apart from the delicate issue of whether new research should go
on, there is the question of what to do with the artifacts and skeletal
remains that have already been excavated. Mrs. Carter and the Caddo
want some of the material returned, but this too raises some of the
conflicts and compromises that her job is full of. For one, she would
like to have Caddoan artifacts housed near the tribal center in Binger,
Oklahoma, but as yet the tribe does not have the substantial and expensive museum facilities it would need. In a video presentation titled "Caddo Thoughts on Repatriation," Mrs. Carter commented,

> The hurt is that so few of our Caddo people have ever been able to see
> those things, because most of them are stored in museums that are dis-
> tant from our local area. And so except for a relatively small number of
> us who have been able to travel to those places and visit them and see
> those things, no one knows about them. . . . And it's particularly sad
> that our young people, most of our young people, have never seen those
> gorgeous pots, the beautiful vessels and the vases, the points with all
> that marvelous [flint] knapping and all of those lovely artifacts. Our
> young people don't know that their ancestors made things of such in-
> trinsic beauty. And so they're missing out on a pride in their heritage
> that they should have the opportunity to know about.

Mrs. Carter is working with some of the large museums with Caddoan collections to send traveling exhibits to the Caddo Culture Center. Even doing this involves some conflict, however, because with
most Caddo she feels that "these are Caddo things and they should be-
long to Caddo people." She does not feel the Caddo should have to ask
to borrow back things that they already consider to be their own.

Until a few years ago, that feeling of ownership toward artifacts
and skeletal remains would not have carried much legal weight. This

changed, however, in 1990, when Congress passed Public Law 101-601, the Native American Graves Protection and Repatriation Act, or NAGPRA. NAGPRA has changed a lot of things about how federal agencies and museums deal with Native American material. For one thing, the legislation substantially agrees with the Caddo concerning the ownership of Caddoan burial goods. As it appears in NAGPRA's legalese,

> If . . . the cultural affiliation of Native American human remains and associated funerary objects with a particular Indian tribe or Native Hawaiian organization is established, then the Federal agency or museum, upon the request of a known lineal descendant of the Native American or of the tribe or organization and pursuant to subsections (b) and (e) of this section, shall expeditiously return such remains and associated funerary objects.

Many things that appear fairly clear in NAGPRA are a lot more complex in practice. Exactly how, for instance, does one determine the "cultural affiliation" of objects or skeletal remains? And even if this can be done with some degree of certainty, how can one know who is a "lineal descendant"? The nature of the Euroamerican conquest of North America was such that some historical groups have no lineal descendants. Who then speaks for the last of the Mohicans? (Actually, with apologies to James Fenimore Cooper, there are quite a few modern Mohicans to speak for their forebears.) Who speaks for the Clovis hunters and gatherers who colonized so widely more than 10,000 years ago? Their descendants may include all Native Americans or none at all.

NAGPRA is the sort of complicated, loosely woven legislation that raises labyrinthine difficulties in interpretation. The more it tries to be specific about matters, the looser it becomes. Perhaps this problem is inherent in any attempt to link archaeological remains of ancient people with modern people along historical paths that are in most cases undocumented and impossible to trace. Perhaps it is so difficult because the law tries to deal directly with the elusive quality of ethnic identity—does the essence of what it is to be ethnically Irish or Oneida or Chechen survive the centuries and pass down intact through dozens of generations? (Under U.S. law it can for Native Americans, but only if a rather arcane set of criteria, involving the continuous existence of a community, with leadership and in some cases a written constitution, is met.) But right now, in museums and tribal councils across the country, the specifics of repatriation are falling to Native Americans and archaeologists who must sit down together and sort out the details of how NAGPRA will be implemented. And in most cases the decisions will not fall to those whose rhetoric is loudest, but to the people who have been stuck with the enormous amount of work NAGPRA involves. Across the country, archaeologists and tribal representatives are having to talk things over and come to agreements case by case.

This new reality and need to find common ground has changed the relationship between the two groups. Despite the popular perception to the contrary, archaeologists and Native Americans often enjoy fairly good relations. There are issues that divide them, such as whether human skeletal remains excavated in the past should be reburied, but also interests held in common, such as the desire to learn more about how people lived in the past. It is also clear that the two have a common enemy. While Native Americans and archaeologists debate legalities and interpretations of NAGPRA, looters are using backhoes to mine ancient sites and cemeteries for artifacts. In some states, if the sites are on private land, it is perfectly legal. Looters and unregulated property development will obliterate more archaeological sites in a year than archaeologists ever have or ever will. The sad truth may be that archaeologists and Indians are uneasy allies in a losing battle to defend the remains of the past.

At the Caddo Conference, as is the case at many large meetings, most of the really important communication happens around the coffeepot during the breaks. Darrell Creel, an archaeologist who has worked on Caddoan prehistory for a long time and who is the curator of collections at a large archaeological repository, was talking with Mrs. Carter. They had known each other and had gotten along well for years. I only heard part of the conversation, but they had to come to some decision about what was to be done with some of the material in the collections. It had long since been decided that the material in question was going back to the Caddo, but there were complicated matters of when and how. None of the complex issues involving the Native American skeletal remains and associated grave goods has an easy or obvious resolution. As in each case decisions have to be made about what to do with particular collections, it is perhaps best that it comes down to a continuing dialogue, at a local and personal level, between archaeologists and tribal representatives (and not the Native American/museological version of the Simpson trial). Over coffee that morning the decisions about how NAGPRA would be implemented were calmly being made. As they parted, I heard them leave things as, "I'll call you Monday morning, we'll sort it out."

Works Cited and Suggestions for Further Reading

American Indian Ritual Object Repatriation Foundation (web site)
http://www.repatriationfoundation.org/

Carter, Cecile Elkins
1995   *Caddo Indians: Where We Come from*. Norman: University of Okla-
            homa Press.

Lippert, Dorothy Thompson
1992   *Skeletons in Our Closets: Archaeology and the Issue of Reburial*. Master's
            thesis, Department of Anthropology, University of Texas at
            Austin.

Native American Grave Protection and Repatriation Act of 1990
(NAGPRA)(web sites)
Information on NAGPRA can be found on ARCHNET at the University of
Connecticut: http://archnet.uconn.edu/
and also at the National Park Service's National Archaeological Database
pages at: http://www.cast.uark.edu/other/nps/nagpra/

Perttula, Timothy K.
1992   *The Caddo Nation: Archaeological and Ethnohistoric Perspectives*.
            Austin: University of Texas Press.

Swindler, N., K. Dongoske, R. Anyon, and A. Downer (eds.)
1997   *Native Americans and Archaeologists: Stepping Stones to Common
            Ground*. Walnut Creek, CA: AltaMira Press.

A Texas Powwow

It is pouring rain outside the Inn of the Twelve Clans on the Alabama-Coushatta reservation in east Texas, and no one is eager to leave. Because of the rain, the afternoon's gourd dances, which were to have been held in the powwow arena at the community center baseball field, have been moved into the gymnasium. Whenever the restaurant door swings open, the drum can be heard in the distance. The dancing last night had gone on until after midnight, and there was a five-mile run at seven this morning, so more than a few are willing to linger over lunch, saving their energy for the evening's dances.

Jack B., a member of the Alabama tribe, sits at a Formica table and counts through his children and grandchildren. One of his seven children married a Pawnee, one an Omaha, a few married non-Indians. Everything he says is accompanied with quick, strong gestures. "He went away, became an outsider," he says, sweeping his arm toward the restaurant door. (I look.) "But he might come back, maybe to retire," he continues, pointing to his chest. Speaking of an aunt, he presses three fingers hard against his left palm and tells us, "She came back here a couple of years ago, but she died."

As we sit in the inn, the people at the table are constantly coming and going. Jack's son needs car keys. Jack's sister stops by (but is soon called away by a relative). A young woman who lives off the reservation and works for the *Houston Post* drifts by a couple of times. Her T-shirt has a raccoon on it, and several people make the connection—her nickname is *Sawa*, "raccoon" in the Alabama language. John Humano, Sr., one of the powwow (dance ceremony) officials, sits for a while. Someone mistakenly introduces him as a Kiowa Apache and is corrected by a chorus; he is Comanche and his wife is Kiowa. He likes to say he's a "Kiowa captive." As people come and go, the joke is repeated a few more times.

The conversation drifts somehow to languages. English is not Jack's first language or probably his second, as he speaks both Alabama and Coushatta. Maybe it is not even his third, as his mother was half Choctaw and he speaks that tribe's language, too. All of these are languages in the Muskogean family, which includes Creek, Chickasaw, and others spoken by the Native Americans of the Southeast. Jack counts from one to ten in Alabama and then in Choctaw and observes that the number eight is practically the same (*ontotchiina* in Alabama, *untuchina* in Choctaw). He notes that knowing one of the languages makes the others easier, although in his opinion, things in Choctaw are sometimes said backward.

Thirty years ago, someone notes, none of the kids entering first grade spoke any English, so they were often held back a year or two. Jack nods. Now most children know English well by the time they enter school. They also understand Alabama or Coushatta, but many will not use these languages unless they have to when speaking to older people. Even so, much of the discussion taking place at surrounding tables is in Alabama or Coushatta.

At the time of first European contact, the ancestors of the Alabama-Coushatta lived along the major rivers of central Alabama—the Coosa, Tallapoosa, and Alabama. Hernando de Soto must have met some of them in his meandering expedition through the Southeast in the early 1540s. Documents and maps from the early 1700s show the location of "Alibamu" and "Kosati" villages still in this territory. But under increasing pressure from British and other European colonists moving west in the mid-1700s, the Alabama and Coushatta moved to lands in Louisiana and east Texas.

Thus the Alabama and Coushatta were settled in Texas in the late 1700s, before Anglo-American colonization of the region (the battle of the Alamo was in 1836). By the late 1820s, they had asked the Mexican government for permanent possession of their lands, and after Texas became an independent republic in 1836, the well-established and prosperous Alabama and Coushatta were the only groups to be exempted from a purge of Native Americans. They again escaped the fate of so many Indians of the southeastern woodlands,

Sunday School Queen Shaa Pancho riding in the powwow parade.

who were forced to move to the Oklahoma Indian Territories in the 1830s (the Cherokee "trail of tears" was just one such forced relocation). As a result of their unusual history, the Alabama-Coushatta reservation is somewhat isolated from other areas with large Native American populations.

Next to the gymnasium where the dance drum is beating lies the Alabama-Coushatta cemetery, surrounded by the tall pine and oak forest of the Big Thicket, as this part of east Texas is called. Some of the headstones date back to the mid-1800s. Back in the woods is the grave of subchief Colabe Sylestine, who in the nineteenth century helped lead the Alabama and Coushatta to their present home in Polk County and who signed the agreement with the State of Texas granting his people their land. Elsewhere in the cemetery, the short flagstaffs of long-since-dissolved flags lean against the headstone of McConico Batisse (1875–1951), a former chief of the Alabama. A razor, a tin coffee cup, and the shell of a flashlight sit along the line of the grave. The rain has washed away some of the gray sand around them, creating little pedestals for these characteristic possessions of the deceased.

Henry Steel, a Kickapoo from Oklahoma, was master of ceremonies for the first night of dances at the powwow last night. He may have been asked because of his "gift of gab," and rightfully so. He delights in intertribal jokes and camaraderie: "We're going to have three intertribal songs; in my language that's *niiswikwaa*, for you Comanches that's *tres*, and for you Cherokees"—holding up three fingers—"it's this many."

For an hour or more before the grand entry, men, mostly older ones, performed the gourd dances. In front of the improvised benches that enclosed the dance circle, they danced slowly in and out to the music from the singers and drummers; some occasionally paused to shake hands and talk with one another in groups of two or three. They wore different versions of "traditional dress," some simply jeans and a western-cut shirt with a long, narrow sash tied around the waist and another sash over the shoulders. Each carried a feathered fan in his left hand and shook a gourd rattle in his right.

Sitting at the center of the dance circle on metal folding chairs stenciled ACIR (Alabama-Coushatta Indian Reservation), a half dozen men sang and beat a large skin drum. Around them sat three or four women, also singing, and a few restless children who had to stay beside their parents or grandparents. Known collectively as the Drum, the people who sing and beat the drum are the soul of the powwow; they can carry on for hours without breaks.

Meanwhile the dancers for the evening's main ceremonies were getting ready. Some of the powwow dances involve competition in costume and dancing, putting personal status, skill, and grace to the test. For the mostly younger participants in these competitions, the dances also carry overtones of courtship and romance. Some of the evening's most impressive choreography took place in the parking lot as parents, often while dressing themselves, helped their restless children into elaborate outfits with headpieces, moccasins, and other components. The MC chastised everyone for the delay in the grand entry: "We're running late. We're twenty-two minutes into Indian time."

Miraculously—at a time determined by them and not by the MC—the milling horde became an ordered procession. An honor guard of war veterans entered the dance circle first, carrying the flags of the United States and Texas and a flag commemorating MIAs. The head gourd dancer, John Dart (another visitor from Oklahoma), came next, followed by the princesses of the Alabama and Coushatta tribes, both high school seniors. Some other "royalty" followed. The women in buckskin regalia entered next, then women wearing "southern shawl costume," or "southern cloth dress"—silk or satin dresses in muted blues and reds, with bonework or beadwork draped over their shoulders and hanging down in front and back, a tasseled shawl over their left arm, and a feather fan in their right hand. Next came women in "northern shawl costume," a similar dress, but with the tasseled shawl unfolded and draped over their shoulders, a style more suited to exuberant dances favored by the younger women. Others wore "jingle dresses" covered with hundreds of shiny metal bells.

The men followed in "traditional dress," a diverse category of regalia that usually included a three-foot circle of tail feathers worn behind the hips. They wore moccasins, a breechcloth, a headdress of fur or a few upright feathers, bonework or colored beadwork, breastplates, armbands, legbands, and face paint, and usually held a short, ornate staff in the right hand. One man wore a wolfskin cape, with the wolf's head coming out over his forehead. His face was painted with wide, vertical white stripes, and he danced in a distinctive crouching, staccato step.

Then came the "fancy dress" dancers, whose costumes were flamboyant elaborations on the men's traditional dress. Their dance was the most athletic of all, and their regalia were designed to amplify every movement. In addition to the bustle of tail feathers, they had another circle of feathers around their shoulders, all of them tipped with streamers. The feathers and other parts of the costumes were

The Drum—drummers and singers—in the powwow parade.

dyed in brilliant colors. Sequined shoes, neon colors, and chromed bonework showed that innovative decorations were not discouraged.

Now, dyed feathers, beadwork, bone breastplates, and huge bustles of feathers were admittedly not part of Alabama or Coushatta dress in centuries past. Some of the tedious cognoscenti of the powwow circuit lament this loss of tradition and deride the incorporation of Plains Indian dress as well as completely novel styles. But so what if these are not the sorts of clothes the ancestors of the Alabama and Coushatta wore? People of European ancestry no longer wear powdered wigs, knee breeches, or big-buckled shoes. Why should the distinctive powwow costumes, one of the most exuberant expressions of Native American creativity, be held to any different standard?

After the grand entry came the "tiny tots" competitions. Their regalia were something like that of the older participants, but with Mickey Mouse disposable diapers instead of breechcloths. Things slowed a bit, with feathered headpieces slipping down over eyes, and armbands and sashes being shed as fast as parents could put them on.

Quite a few of the spectators wandered over to the booths to get something to eat. Frybread is a staple on the Alabama-Coushatta reservation, and on the powwow circuit generally. It is bread dough formed into a thin slab about five inches across, then slipped into a frying pan of hot oil. The result is something like a chewy, unsweetened doughnut without a hole. Topped with beans, cheese, and lettuce, it becomes an "Indian taco."

After a few other competitive classes came the ladies' southern shawl dance, a subtle exercise that lacks the spinning and shaking of the fancy dancers. This contest had the most dancers, spanning the greatest range of ages, with women in their fifties and sixties competing with those in their teens. The drum started and the dancers moved slowly forward, clockwise, as if walking carefully through the dark, trying to see who was there or to find something they lost. The tassels of the folded shawls draped over the dancers' left arms raked back and forth, and the beadwork down their backs swept back and forth to the same rhythm. In her motionless right hand, elbow bent, each dancer held a feather fan. After three great beats on the drum they danced lower, the fringes of their shawls nearly touching the ground. Two songs were needed for all the southern shawl dancers to compete.

Among the evening's dances, the most exciting was the Tracy Batisse Memorial Competition for male fancy dancers. At smaller powwows during the year, the dancers had competed to get into the finals for this competition, the prestige of which far exceeds the $1,000 cash, silk jacket, and other prizes that come with winning. The four finalists all seemed to be about eighteen to twenty years old. They had been wandering around behind the bleachers for the previous half hour, stretching, looking up in the air, turning away friends who wanted to talk, and shaking their shoulders and fingers like sprinters waiting for their call to the blocks.

About 2,000 people were watching the dances, the majority of them Indians. About 500 were Alabama and Coushatta living on the reservation; perhaps another 1,000 lived away but had come back for the annual powwow. Other Native Americans present included Chickasaw, Cherokee, Choctaw, Seminole, and Creek from Oklahoma and, from farther away, Sac, Fox, Comanche, Kiowa, Lakota, and Shoshone. Many non-Indians had also come, some from neighboring towns and some from great distances, to enjoy the dancing and the welcoming atmosphere of the powwow.

No one was getting frybread now. The MC called for a "contest dance," and the Drum started off at an exhilarating pace. The fancy dancers shook the tassels streaming from their shoulders and hips, spinning the tasseled batons looped around their wrists. Leaping and turning, they looked like a flurry of feathers. They danced the same dance, but each added his own new moves. Girlfriends and family sat around the dance arena, arched forward, clenching their fists.

The Drum's rapid pace slowed for three intense beats, and with them the dancers all flew downward into a low crouch, jumping three times. The participants' passion, and the focused hush of the crowd, made it plain that this was no show for tourists. The annual powwow is the event all the Alabama and Coushatta try to come home for, and this dance is its centerpiece. The dancers are competitive, to be sure, but together they reflect a commitment to Alabama and Coushatta identity and tradition.

The Drum then launched into a furious tempo, taking the dancers with it. Finally the Drum ended the song with a great flourish, leaving the four finalists reaching for the sky, dripping sweat and exhausted, feathers quivering and tasseled batons twirling high above from both wrists. A storm of applause burst from the crowd, as the MC quipped, "Well, gentlemen, that was a good warm-up song—now let's start the competition!"

Works Cited and Suggestions for Further Reading

Alabama-Coushatta Indian Reservation (web site)
Information on the Alabama-Coushatta http://www.livingston.net/
chamber/actribe/index.htm

Hook, Jonathan B.
1997   *The Alabama-Coushatta Indians.* College Station: Texas A & M University Press.

Powwow Highway
1989   A film by Handmade Films. Executive producers, George Harrison and Denis O'Brien. Based on the novel by David Seals. Published by Cannon Video, 91 min.

Southern Native American Pow Wows (web site)
Information on schedules, resources, etc. http://tqd.advanced.org/3081/

Trickster Treats

In the tall mountains and forests of the Northwest, before the Whites came, and even before the advent of the Real People—the Nee Mee Poo, or Nez Perce—Coyote lived there. The Nez Perce of Idaho and the northern Rockies tell how their very existence is owed to the cleverness of Coyote, the legendary trickster of Native American folk tradition:

> Long before there were any people on the earth, a huge monster came down from the North, eating every animal he could find. He ate all the animals, from the smallest to the largest, from mice to mountain lions, all except Coyote, the trickster. Coyote could not find any of his friends, and this made him mad. So he crossed the Snake River and climbed the highest mountain. He tied himself to its peak with a stout rope and challenged the monster to try to eat him. The monster tried to suck Coyote from his perch, but the rope was too strong. Suspecting that Coyote was more clever than he, the monster befriended Coyote and asked him to come stay with him.
>
> One day Coyote asked the monster if he could go into his stomach and visit all the animals the monster had eaten, and the monster agreed. Once inside, Coyote told his friends to get ready to escape. He took out his fire starter and built a huge fire in the belly of the monster. Then he took his knife and cut out the monster's head. All the animals escaped.
>
> In honor of the defeat of the monster, Coyote said that he would create a new animal. He cut the monster into pieces and flung them in all directions; where each piece landed—on the plains, along the rivers, and on the mountains of North America—a tribe of Indians sprang up. When he had finished, Coyote's friend Fox observed that no tribe was born on the spot where Coy-

ote had killed the monster. Coyote was sad because of this omission, but he had no more monster parts. Then he had an idea. He washed the monster's blood from his hands and let the drops fall on the ground. Coyote said, "Here on this ground I make the Nez Perce. They will be few in number, but they will be strong and pure." And this is how the human beings came to be. (retold from "Coyote Makes Human Beings," Lopez 1977)

Trickster tales are the most widespread form of Native American folktale. The trickster most often is the coyote or rabbit, but sometimes he is a spider, as among the Oglala Dakota. Whatever he is called, his name has only a little to do with his character, which is an amalgam of the characteristics of his animal namesake, humans, and supernatural beings.

The trickster tale is not just a Native American phenomenon: It is found in folklore or mythology throughout the world. In Greek mythology, Prometheus and his brother Epimetheus possess both the trickster's cunning and his foolishness, as does Hermes. In Polynesia, Maui the trickster makes rope of his sister's hair to lasso and slow down Ra, the sun. The spider Ananse is the trickster among the Ashanti of Africa: An enormous class of their trickster tales is simply called *anansesem,* or "spider stories," regardless of whether Ananse appears in them. Among the Azande people of central Africa the trickster is a spider as well: Ture is an animal so clever he can make a web out of himself. But the anthropologist E. E. Evans-Pritchard, in his classic *Zande Trickster,* speaks of the complexities and contradictions in the trickster's character, calling Ture

> a monster of depravity: liar, cheat, lecher, murderer; vain greedy, treacherous, ungrateful, a poltroon, a braggart. This utterly selfish person is everything against which Azande warn their children most strongly. Yet he is the hero of their stories, and it is to their children that his exploits are related and he is presented, with very little moralizing—if as a rogue, as an engaging one. For there is another side to his character, which even to us is appealing: his whimsical fooling, recklessness, impetuosity, puckish irresponsibility, his childish desire to show how clever he is . . . and his flouting of every convention. In spite of his nefarious conduct he is never really malicious. Indeed he has an endearing innocence.

Like most myths and folktales, the trickster tales encode varying values and ideas, and some of these are specific to particular cultures.

Brer Rabbit visits Brer Fox (from Joel Chandler Harris, His Songs and His Sayings. *Courtesy of the Perry Casteñeda Library).*

Yet the same themes are played out in strikingly similar ways throughout the world, because the trickster tales deal with issues of universal human experience—family interactions, competition, struggles against authority, love, and death. The many sides to the trickster's personality make him especially useful to the storyteller: Some tales emphasize the trickster's spiritual side and others his material side; some his role as creator and some as mean-spirited destroyer. The psychologist Carl Jung saw in the trickster a primordial figure who transcends humankind's conceptual boundaries between gods and mortals, who moves freely between the worlds of gods and humans and plays tricks on both.

Many stories capture the trickster as the primal comedian, able to step outside of a situation (or a culture) and point out its ridiculousness. The trickster is incarnated in Shakespeare's Puck of *A Midsummer Night's Dream* and in cartoons ("Twicky wabbit" is what Elmer

Fudd calls Bugs Bunny, a classic trickster if ever there was one). Bart Simpson's constant challenge to authority qualifies him for the trickster role.

Trickster tales often serve to entertain and instruct children, teaching them how to behave and how the world works. In Native American stories, as elsewhere, the trickster is often the underdog, never the most powerful or beautiful animal. The trickster is the one who through cleverness defeats more powerful forces, using their very superiority, arrogance, or vanity as a weapon against them. The story of Possum's tail warns against such hubris, as in this version, which combines elements of similar stories told throughout eastern North America:

> Possum was proud of his long, bushy tail; he took great pleasure in combing it out every day, and especially in waving it in front of Coyote (whose own tail was scraggly and flea-bitten). When the Animal People came together for council and a big dance, Possum demanded a special seat so that everyone could see his beautiful tail. Coyote agreed to this, and told Possum that he would even send Cricket over to comb out his tail before the dance.

> Before sending him to help Possum primp, Coyote had a talk with Cricket (who was the best barber among the Animal People). Cricket went and spent hours brushing out Possum's tail, and when he was done he carefully wrapped the tail in a red thread and said, "Possum, this string will keep all the hairs in place until the dance. When you get to the council and it's time to dance then you can take the string off."

> Possum went to the lodge where the dance was held and took his place of honor in the middle of the Animal People. When the drummers began, Possum removed the thread and began to dance in the middle of the lodge. "See my beautiful tail," he said, as everyone began to snicker. He said, "See how fine the fur is," while Coyote nearly wept trying to contain himself. "See how it sweeps the ground," he said, as all the Animal People roared in laughter. Finally Possum looked around at his naked, scaly tail. He rolled onto his back and grinned, as he does to this day when he's caught by surprise. (retold from Radin 1956)

Although trickster tales may warn against vanity, greed, and excessive cleverness, they are also highly entertaining, which helps to account for their wide distribution and longevity. The similarities in trickster stories drawn from African American and Native American folktales are apparent in the following examples. The first features one of the most famous tricksters known to contemporary Americans—Brer Rabbit, whose roots lie in West African folktale traditions. In "How Brother Fox Was Too Smart," as in many trickster tales, Brer Rabbit uses Fox's conceit to bring him down:

> Walking with Fox one day, Brer Rabbit saw a track that Brer Fox did not recognize. When Fox asked what it was, Rabbit said, "If I'm not mistaken, the poor creature who made that track is Cousin Wildcat, no more and no less." "How big is he, Brer Rabbit," Fox asked. "He's about your size." Then Brer Rabbit acted like he was talking to himself, "Tut, tut, tut! It's funny that I should come across Cousin Wildcat in this part of the world. Many's the time I saw my Grandaddy kick and cuff Cousin Wildcat, so much so that I felt sorry for him. If you want any fun, Brer Fox, now's the time to get it." Brer Fox, who fancied himself a fighter, was interested; he asked Brer Rabbit how he was going to have fun with the Wildcat. "It's easy enough. Just go tackle ole Cousin Wildcat and slam him around. . . . Just hit him a good one, and if he tries to run away, I'll catch him for you."

The climax of the story is predictable enough, with Rabbit coaxing Fox into an unwise battle:

> In short order, Fox was lying on the ground in pieces crying, "I'm ruined, Brer Rabbit! I'm ruined! Run get the doctor, I'm totally ruined!" Brer Rabbit headed home and when he got out of sight, he bent over and shook his hands like a cat does when she gets water on her feet, and he laughed and laughed until he was nearly sick from laughing. (retold from Harris 1881)

In a similar confrontation, the two great tricksters of North America—Coyote and Rabbit—attempt to outsmart each other:

> One day Coyote came upon Rabbit, who was making a strong leather sack. He asked, "What is that sack for, Rabbit?" Rabbit replied, "A hailstorm is coming, and I'm making this sack to protect myself." "Rabbit," said Coyote, "give me this sack and make yourself another one, so that we can both be safe." Coyote climbed into the sack and Rabbit hung him in a tree. Making sounds like a violent storm, Rabbit pelted the sack with rocks. When Coyote stuck his head out and saw that the hailstorm was only Rabbit

throwing rocks, he was very angry. He chased Rabbit, who had gone to a field where crops were growing. Rabbit's curiosity was aroused by a stick figure in the field covered with sticky gum. When Rabbit touched it, his finger became stuck, and the more he tried to work himself free, the more stuck he became. Finally Coyote arrived, still angry. "Rabbit, before I kill you, tell me what you are doing stuck to that pole." Thinking fast, Rabbit replied, "The person whose crops these are wants me to share a feast with him, but I don't want to do it. He says that after I've been stuck to this pole for a while, I'll be hungry enough to share his great meal." So Coyote pulled Rabbit loose and stuck himself to the pole. When the angry farmer returned, Coyote paid the price.

Now Coyote was so angry he was biting his tongue and walking into rocks. When he found Rabbit again he said, "Now I am going to kill you before you can say another word." Rabbit was sitting in front of a beehive, and he gestured for Coyote to be quiet. "Be quiet, Coyote, I am teaching these small children, and afterwards they will repay me with a meal." Coyote couldn't see into the hive, and did not recognize it for what it was. But he thought that he could finally outsmart Rabbit. "Let me teach the children for a while, Rabbit, while you rest. By the way, how will they know when it is time to serve up your meal?" Rabbit replied, "When it is dinner time you must hit the hive with this club until they come out. You must hit it very hard, because they do not hear very well." Coyote lectured to the humming hive for a long while. He told of what a great warrior he was and of the great battles he had fought. Finally he began to get hungry. He looked around to make sure that Rabbit was out of sight, and then took the club and hit the hive so hard that it broke in two. (retold from Radin 1956)

In these two tales both Rabbit and Coyote (or Fox) are tricksters, and in turn they show their mixture of artful finesse and bumbling stupidity. They beat their heads together and produce entertaining stories that have been successful for ages. But in doing so they transmit basic truths about the human condition.

In the Winnebago stories of the trickster called Hare, the ambiguous hero decides to help out the human beings and makes all the animals defenseless against them. But when he returns to the lodge of his grandmother (who in this cycle of stories represents the earth herself), he finds that although he has cleverly achieved what he wanted, outsmarting each of the animals in turn, the result does more harm than good:

Hare thought to himself, "Now the people will live peacefully and forever." But the old woman, his grandmother, said, "Grandson, your talk makes me sad. How can the people live forever, as you do? Earthmaker did not make them thus. All things have to have an end. You yourself in your travels around the country must have seen trees fallen to the ground. That is their end—that is their death. Everything will have an end. I also will have an end as I am created that way." Then Hare looked in her direction and some of her back caved in just as the earth does sometimes. That was what he saw. And he saw people cave in with the earth. "Grandson, thus it is," said the old woman, "I have been created small and if all the people live forever they would soon fill up the earth. There would then be more suffering than there is now, for some people would always be in want of food if they multiplied greatly. That is why everything has an end." Then Hare thought for a long time. "A good thing I had obtained for the people, but my grandmother has spoiled it." So he felt sad, took his blanket, covered himself with it, lay down in the corner and wept. (retold from Radin 1956)

Works Cited and Suggestions for Further Reading

Erdoes, Richard, and Alfonso Ortiz (eds.)
1998   *American Indian Trickster Tales.* New York: Viking.

Evans-Pritchard, E. E.
1967   *Zande Trickster.* Oxford, UK: Clarendon Press.

Gidley, M.
1981   *Kopet: A Documentary Narrative of Chief Joseph's Last Years.* Seattle: University of Washington Press.

Harris, Joel Chandler
1881   *Nights with Uncle Remus.* London: G. Routledge.

Lopez, Barry Holstun
1977   *Giving Birth to Thunder, Sleeping with His Daughter.* Kansas City: Sheed Andrews & McMeel.

Radin, Paul
1956   *The Trickster.* London: Routledge & Kegan Paul.

Index